VODKA

Shake, Muddle, Stir

Vodka: Shake, Muddle, Stir by Dan Jones

First published in 2019 by Hardie Grant Books,
an imprint of Hardie Grant Publishing

Hardie Grant Books (UK)
52–54 Southwark Street
London SE1 1UN

Hardie Grant Books (Australia)
Ground Floor, Building 1
658 Church Street
Melbourne, VIC 3121

hardiegrantbooks.com

British Library Cataloguing-in-Publication Data. A catalogue record
for this book is available from the British Library.

ISBN: 978-1-78488-249-5

Publishing Director: Kate Pollard
Junior Editor: Eila Purvis
Art Direction: Matt Phare
Illustrator: Daniel Servansky
Copy editor: Kay Delves
Proofreader: Emily Preece-Morrison
Indexer: Cathy Heath
Colour Reproduction by p2d

Printed and bound in China by Leo Paper Group

VODKA

Shake, Muddle, Stir

by Dan Jones

ILLUSTRATIONS BY DANIEL SERVANSKY

Hardie Grant

BOOKS

CONTENTS

Welcome

to

VODKA

Shake, Muddle, Stir

TAKE YOUR MEDICINE

In ages past, vodka was a mysterious cure-all, a magic potion administered to break fevers, clean wounds, warm your chilliest bits and mend broken hearts; its power was immense. Eastern Europe was in thrall to the clear, powerful spirit (much like England's cross-eyed love affair with gin) and it very nearly brought Russia to its knees when workers were struck with rising bar debts and horror hangovers. Then came the vodka diaspora, when makers like Pyotr Smirnov introduced the spirit to Parisian intellectuals and racy US bar owners, and soon vodka took up its hallowed place on cocktail lists all over the world.

This is *Vodka: Shake, Muddle, Stir*, your starter in how to mix it, shake it, stir it and – most importantly – how to drink it. A celebration of the finest vodka the world has to offer, with a little history, some tried-and-tested international brands and blends, and a tour through the equipment, gadgets and techniques needed to make the very best vodka drinks. Then, the recipes themselves: classics to master and new-found flavours to experiment with. Perhaps the science of booze-making has made us less superstitious about the power of vodka, but its magic has never waned.

Dan Jones

THE BEST MEDICINE

No one, it seems, can agree on the true birthplace of vodka. Is it Russia? Poland? Sweden? For all the claims on the spirit's true nationality, one thing is clear: the history of Eastern Europe is soaked in it.

Most agree that *aqua vitae*, the hellish potion popular in the Middle Ages, is the inspiration behind vodka's first incarnation. Trade routes took the distilled grape hooch east, where it was presented to Polish dignitaries and Russian princes as a powerful pick-me-up. In fact, vodka's history of medicinal use has lodged in the subconsciousness of Eastern Europe. It's still thought of as a cure-all, staving off the cold, bringing down a fever and disinfecting cuts and grazes.

Soon, homegrown aqua vitae-like medicinal spirits grew in popularity, with makers swapping out grape wine for fermented grains or potatoes. Records from the 1400s suggest a monk, based in the Moscow Kremlin, came up with his own rather tantalising vodka recipe; many Polish vodka blends date back centuries; and the spirit has been produced in Sweden since the late fifteenth century.

By the sixteenth century, vodka was no longer just a medicine, but a delicious drink that powered the working class.

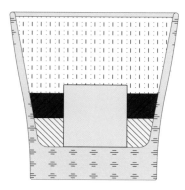

By the seventeenth century, batch distillation meant the spirit was more plentiful (if not a little murky), and in Russia, tavern owners would distil their own for a thirsty clientele. Vodka-mania took hold and soon workers, farmers and party animals found themselves mired in debt to the taverns. The Church and State tried to curb vodka's popularity, restricting its production, until Tsar Alexander III decided to improve the spirit, curing both the hangovers and debts of vodka's most dedicated fans. Chemist Dmitri Mendeleev tweaked the recipe, fixing the alcohol content at 40 per cent, and based the amounts of water and alcohol used to make vodka on volume rather than weight

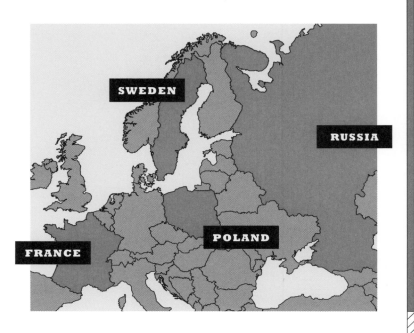

– a form that other vodka countries soon adopted. In fact, the vodka we know and love today has changed very little over the past 250 years, not since the Russian discovery that charcoal (rather than felt or sand) could be used to purify the spirit. That, plus Mendeleev's original tweaks, created a clear, powerful drop.

Vodka's sophisticated international rep can be traced back to just after the 1917 Russian Revolution, when Lenin halted private vodka production, closed distilleries and forced vodka producers out of the country. One of those producers, Pyotr Smirnov, moved to Paris. He rebranded, changing his name to Pierre Smirnoff, and introduced Parisians to his new, startlingly powerful spirit. More brands emerged in the 1930s and 40s, finding their way into classic drinks like the Moscow Mule and Bloody Mary, and vodka became a world-class spirit. Together, we drink more than 4.4 billion litres of it each year, knowing that it will add a clean, smooth power

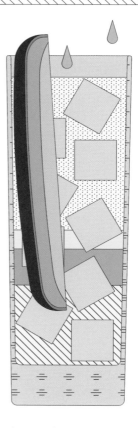

punch to our favourite drinks, make awkward social engagements run a little smoother, and perhaps leave us more than a little merry; vodka has always been the best medicine.

VODKA: THE SCIENCE BIT

In the vodka world, pure means perfect. The world's leading vodka makers lean heavily on the idea of their spirit's clean, crisp taste, apparently achieved through all manner of fancy filtration systems (charcoal, garnets, quartz – even diamonds), the millions of times it's distilled, or the use of glacial water as rare as unicorn tears. But the more you filter, distil and dilute something, the less flavour it might have, and so a rather careful balance must be achieved.

Vodka's most important element, ethanol, has been made for thousands of years. Yeast and sugar from fruit or grains ferment into a murky mess from which ethanol can be extracted. But it's this murky mess (created by the fruit or grains) that gives vodka its flavour profile. A strict distillation process does indeed make a purer and smoother drop, but how to create a spirit that has the perfect purity/flavour ratio? That's where the magic happens: vodka makers' secret distillation processes, developed over centuries, make sure each bottle of spirit is as pure as possible without a loss of its flavoursome impurities. Luckily, the flavour molecules are tough little guys and hard to completely remove, but the resulting spirit – after distillation – generally has a clear, clean, almost neutral taste. That's why vodka is so versatile, accentuating the delicate flavours of other spirits, turning up the volume on the tang of lime juice or earthiness of coffee, in the same way as salt underlines the flavours of food.

The World's Best Vodkas

TRIED AND TESTED: FROM THE FINEST BRIGHT, CLEAN PREMIUM BRANDS FOR PERFECT MIXING TO SINGLE ESTATE SIPPERS, AND SASSY LITTLE FLAVOURED NUMBERS, FROM ALL FOUR CORNERS OF THE GLOBE.

BEST FOR CLASSICISTS

STOLICHNAYA

This little firecracker created from Latvian wheat is blended with glacial water, charcoal filtered and distilled – count 'em – four times, making it smooth-as-velvet with a light peppery, buttery taste. The original red-label Stolichnaya is perfect, but its delicate flavoured versions, from classic Razberi to Blueberi, and premium Elit, are all delicious.

BEST FOR PREMIUM SIPPERS

ABSOLUT ELYX

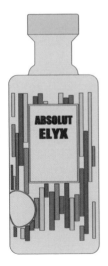

Award-winning Elyx is Absolut's handmade, premium small batch vodka, distilled in a vintage 19212 copper still using wheat from Sweden's Råbelöf estate. The effort – extraordinary for a vodka megabrand – has paid off, as Elyx has a rich, full flavour with a smooth and mellow texture. Swedish Absolut has created vodka since 1877 and its flavoured versions, from Citron to Mandarin, are perfectly balanced and delicious with tonic or soda water.

BEST FOR AFTERNOON TEA

CHASE MARMALADE

Chase is the British craft vodka and gin brand powered by potatoes (and occasionally, apples). The Chasers use Seville orange marmalade in their copper still to infuse this delicious spirit, giving it an orange tone and subtle bitter-sweet taste that's unbelievably tasty. Chase Farm has been in the potato business for more than 20 years and their range of flavoured vodkas is completely unique.

BEST FOR DILL DEVOTEES

GUSTAV DILL VODKA

For more than 165 years, the craftspeople at Finnish distillery Gustav have proudly produced a small range of multi award-winning liqueur, gin and vodka using raw, organic botanicals plucked (sustainably) from the Artic. With a delicious core vodka plus a fruity blueberry version, Gustav's dill vodka is handcrafted from wheat, passed through the distillery's aroma still for a rich dill note. Fairly dry-tasting with a subtle spiciness, no wonder Gustav Dill Vodka is an award-winning spirit (and one of the world's best spirits for making a vodka and tonic).

BEST FOR NIGHTHAWKS

CÎROC

Newcomer Cîroc is the young French upstart produced from Gaillac and Cognac grapes, harvested when frozen, then cold-fermented into wine (because, French) and distilled no less than five times. Because of its extraordinary production (and weighty bottle) Cîroc is considered a super-premium drop; found in the world's best late-night clubs. It's soft with a moderate burn and subtly sweet grapiness.

BEST FOR SMOOTH OPERATORS

GREY GOOSE

The Goose's elite reputation, appearing on the drinks lists of the world's poshest venues since the 1990s, is well deserved. This French grain-based vodka mixed with spring water (naturally filtered through Champagne limestone) has notes of charcoal, pepper and liquorice. In 1998, Grey Goose was named the world's 'Best Tasting' vodka by the Beverage Tasting Institute, and the Goose has never looked back. Soft, smooth and incredibly mellow, a quality amplified by pouring straight from the freezer. Creamy AF.

BEST FOR LEATHER LOVERS

TOM OF FINLAND VODKA

Danish craft booze brand, One Eyed Spirits, is known for its eyebrow-raising inspirations. One Eye's vodka is no exception: it celebrates the life and art of Touko Laaksonen, aka Tom of Finland, with a refined organic wheat and rye spirit blended with Artic spring water.

Since the 1950s, Laaksonen's iconic, homoerotic artworks of musclebound bikers with chiselled jaws and bulging nether regions have influenced contemporary style, culture, eroticism, and now: booze. This spirit, featuring Laaksonen's artwork on the bottle, is as smooth as a leather jockstrap with a premium taste.

BEST FOR CRAFT LOVERS

SMIRNOFF BLACK LABEL

Age-old vodka maker Smirnoff is one of the world's most popular and ubiquitous brands, with its classic red label spirit an easy, inexpensive drop. Smirnoff Black Label is something a little different: a rather special premium vodka, copper pot-distilled and filtered through seven tons of Siberian birch charcoal, in a handcrafted production designed to create the world's most mellow vodka. Smooth and supple.

BEST FOR WANNABE ROYALS

ZUBROWKA

Zubrowka is the king of Polish vodkas, flavoured with a special kind of aromatic bison grass grown wild in the heart of Bialowieza Forest and harvested by hand. Rye-based, Zubrowka has a verdant, creamy flavour with moderate burn and, although delicious as a sipper over ice, it's best in a simple two- to three- ingredient cocktail or with a high-quality mixer, especially apple juice or ginger beer.

BEST FOR SHEEP LOVERS

HARTSHORN DISTILLERY SHEEP WHEY

Young Tasmanian devil Ryan Hartshorn is just what the vodka industry needs: a handsome provocateur who is willing to experiment and push the spirit to the next level. His Sheep Whey Vodka is just that, a labour of love using a by-product from his family's cheese business to create a caramel, fruity vodka that won 'Best Vodka' at the World Vodka Awards 2018.

Essential Vodka Gadgetry

THEY SAY A WORKMAN IS ONLY AS GOOD AS
HIS TOOLS. PUT TOGETHER YOUR OWN GLEAMING
BAR KIT OF ESSENTIAL GADGETS.

IMPRESSIVE TOOLS

Invest in your own at-home cocktail bar with a range of impressive drink-making tools. Start off simple: a shaker, jigger, muddler, bar spoon, strainer, an ice bucket and a wealth of premium vodka. Here's what you'll need to keep it minimal:

JIGGER

A toolbox essential. The jigger is the standard measure for spirits and liqueurs and is available in many different sizes. Heavy metallic jiggers look the part, but plastic or glass versions also do the job. If you don't have a jigger, or a single shot glass as a stand-in, use an egg cup – at least then your ratios will be right, even if your shots might be a little over-generous. Failing that, cross your fingers and free-pour your drinks.

2oz (60ml)

1.5oz (44ml)

MIXING GLASS

A simple, sturdy straight-sided glass (also known as a Boston) – or a straight-sided pint glass that tapers out – used for cocktails that need stirring with a bar spoon rather than shaking or to allow for extra volume when attached to the can of your shaker (to make two or more drinks at a time). The two halves are locked together and you shake until the drink is chilled, then a Hawthorne strainer can be used to strain the drink into a glass.

SHAKER

Sometimes known as the Boston Shaker, it's the home mixer's silver bullet. This is your single most important piece of kit as very few cocktails are possible without one. The classic metallic model has three main parts: a base, known as the 'can' (a tall, tumbler shape that tapers out), a tight-fitting funnel top with built-in strainer, onto which a small cap fits (which can also be used as a jigger). It's brilliantly straightforward, and like all the finest tools, it pays to keep it scrupulously clean. If you can't get your hands on one, consider using a large glass jar with a lid and a waterproof seal.

HAWTHORNE STRAINER

The showy-looking strainer, trimmed with a spring, that comes in handy when your shaker's built-in version isn't up to the job. Place on a glass and pour the cocktail through it, or hold up against the cocktail can or mixing glass and pour from a height. Wash immediately after use, especially if you're straining a cream-based cocktail. A fine tea strainer does the job brilliantly, but the classic Hawthorne really looks the part.

BLENDER

Essential for fruity little numbers. Unless you're using something powerful like a NutriBullet or Vitamix, most domestic blenders find ice a little difficult, so it's best to use crushed ice in blender cocktails, rather than cubes or rocks. Add your ingredients first, then the ice, and start off on a slow speed before turning it up to max. No need to strain. Once the consistency is super-smooth, pour into a glass and serve.

CHOPPING BOARD AND KNIFE

Simple, but essential. Keep the board clean, the knife super sharp and practise your peeling skills: the aim is to avoid as much white pith as possible, leaving just the peel that is studded with aromatic oils.

ICE BUCKET

The centrepiece of your home bar; it can be simple, functional and slightly retro or the full plastic pineapple. An insulated ice bucket means your ice cubes will keep their shape for longer, and a good set of tongs adds a touch of class.

UPSCALE EXTRAS

ICE PICK

Buy bags of filtered, crushed ice or cubes (always buy double or triple the amount that you think you'll need) or attack your own homemade ice block with an ice pick. Boil water, let it cool slightly and pour into an old plastic ice-cream container. Freeze solid, turn out onto a clean tea towel (dish towel), and then attack as needed with a firm grip. The ice will go everywhere, but bear with it. Keep the rocks large and jagged for drinks with a little drama.

CITRUS PRESS

Always, always, always use fresh citrus juices. Never skimp on this part of mixology. If you don't have a lemon squeezer, use your hands. Roll and squish your fruit on a hard surface, slice in half and squeeze through your fingers, catching the pips as you go.

NOVELTY STRAWS, PARASOLS AND PLASTIC MONKEYS

Tricky. Creating hands-down amazing cocktails means that they should taste and look otherworldly just as they are. That's without parasols, plastic monkeys, flashing LED ice cubes and novelty straws you can also wear as glasses. That said, there's something more than a little pleasing about adding the odd frill to your drink. Make sure straws are part of your home bar toolkit – stripy red and white paper ones are pretty eye-catching – and the odd

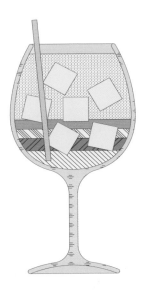

CANELE OR JULIENNE KNIFE

A fancy bit of kit: the canele knife has a V-shaped groove for cutting citrus peel spirals, carving melons and probably many other crafty uses.

COCKTAIL STICK

For spearing cherries, citrus peel, fruit slices, olives, onion slivers, pickles. Sausages, even.

plastic monkey never hurt anyone. Maybe save your penis straws for extra-special occasions like 80th birthday parties.

BAR SPOON

The classic bar spoon has a long, twisted handle, a flat end and a teardrop-shaped spoon used for stirring and measuring out ingredients. It's not essential, but looks pretty cool.

SWIZZLE STICK

More than just cocktail furniture, the swizzle allows the drinker to navigate their own drink, stirring as they go. Great for drinks packed with fruit or garnishes, or for nervous partygoers who need something to fiddle with.

A Guide to Glasses

STEER AWAY FROM USING ORDINARY GLASSWARE
TO SERVE DRINKS. THE HOME MIXER SHOULD
TAKE A LITTLE PRIDE IN WHAT THEY PRESENT
AND INVEST IN SOME UPSCALE COUPES,
TUMBLERS AND HIGHBALLS.

COUPE

The short, trumpet-shaped glass perfect for Champagne and sparkling wines and a respectable martini glass alternative. A vintage coupe is rather special. (**Fig 1**)

MARTINI

Cocktail culture's most iconic glass: the refined stem and cone-shaped glass flares out to create a large, shallow recess. Somehow loses its ability not to slosh out its contents as the evening wears on. (**Fig 2**)

MOSCOW MULE MUG

The iconic copper mug, traditionally used for a Moscow Mule or Mojito. When packed with ice it forms a refreshing-looking frosty condensation.

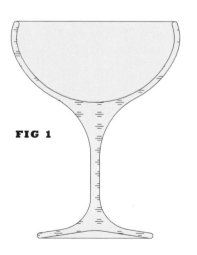

FIG 1

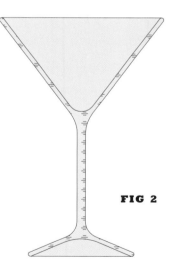

FIG 2

BOSTON GLASS

The twin brother of the straight-sided pint glass, swapped at birth. Great for mixing in or for using locked into the can of your shaker. (**Fig 3**)

SHOT GLASS

Short and simple. Pour, drink, slam down. Done. Also doubles as a jigger.

HIGHBALL

Ostensibly a tall glass, with a thick and sturdy bottom, that holds 225–350 ml (8–12 oz) of perfectly mixed booze. (**Fig 4**)

TUMBLER

The short, straight-sided glass perfect for short or single shot drinks. Like most things, best to pick one with a heavy bottom. (**Fig 5**)

FIG 4

FIG 3

FIG 5

COLLINS GLASS

The skinny, usually straight-sided version of the Highball. (**Fig 6**)

JAM JAR

There are no hard-and-fast rules for how to serve your drinks – or rather what you serve them in. You can use any number of alternatives – jam jars, tea cups, sciencey test tubes and beakers, Russian tea glasses and shoes – to get your guests beyond the pale. (**Fig 7**)

CHAMPAGNE FLUTE

The flute-shaped glass used for Champagne cocktails, Bellinis and Mimosas. (**Fig 8**)

FIG 6

FIG 7

FIG 8

Tricks of the Trade

MASTER THESE SIMPLE RULES TO DRINK BY:
IT'S ALL IN THE TWIST OF THE WRIST.

HOW TO DO IT

HOW TO SHAKE

There's a war going on in cocktail land. How long exactly to shake the perfect concoction? No one can agree. Some say 15 seconds of brisk shaking, others say less. This book is going out on a limb and settles on a short and sharp 7 seconds. Any longer could dilute the drink a little too much, affecting potency. Otherwise, there should be no bottle flipping or sparkler lighting, although a little lemon and lime juggling wouldn't go amiss.

HOW TO STIR

Whip out your bar spoon, and your mixing glass, and stir drinks gently and deftly with ice to chill the concoction. When condensation forms on the outside of the glass, it's ready to go.

HOW TO CHILL

If you have room, clear a shelf in your freezer and keep your cocktail glasses on ice, or pack them full of ice cubes to throw away when the glass is chilled.

POTENCY

All cocktails are potent, but some are more potent than others. Each drink should seek to achieve a perfect balance of flavours and can attempt differing levels of intensity, but shouldn't get you drunk – at least not on its own. Perfect measurements really matter.

THE LOOK

Fresh garnishes, squeaky clean glasses, clear, purified ice and a perfect balance of colours and visible textures are essential.

AROMATICS

Your drink should smell really, really, great – not just taste good. Bitters, fresh juices and citrus peels packed with fragrant oils help achieve this.

HOW TO PUT YOUR BACK BAR TOGETHER

Apart from a collection of the world's best vodkas – from Absolut Extrakt to Stolichnaya – and your own homemade infusions, create a back bar with a mix of strong, clean and classic spirits, the odd special buy, and a few rarities. You don't necessarily need to stock up on fine vintage spirits for cocktail mixing – their subtler qualities are sometimes lost in the mixing – but you do need to invest in something of quality.

VODKA

More of the world's most amazing vodka on pages 12–17. For now, at least invest a little in an upscale number like Absolut or Stolichnaya as your go-to basic.

SYRUP

A cocktail essential. Simple syrup – aka gomme or sugar syrup – is liquid sugar and, mixed part-for-part with sharp citrus juices, brings a delightfully sweet-sour note to a drink. Buy a premium version of simple syrup (Monin is a good, decent brand) or make your own (page 37).

BITTERS

Angostura (Venezuelan-by-way-of-Trinidad-and-Tobago) bitters are an essential element of the back bar. Said to be a cure for hiccups, the part-herbal, part-alcoholic tinctures are highly aromatic, giving cocktails a depth and complexity of taste, and colouring white spirits a subtle sunrise pink. Bitters and cordial

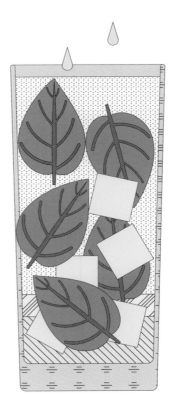

producers Fee Brothers (est. 1863) is another good brand to start with: their whisky barrel-aged bitters with rhubarb and plum flavours are particularly mouth-caving.

GIN

The little 'shot of lightening' has come a long way since its humble beginnings as the demonic hell broth of the London underworld. Handcrafted, premium gins have elevated this powerful spirit to otherworldly proportions. Current star of the gin world? Scottish craft gin, The Botanist.

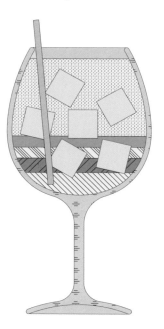

CAMPARI AND APEROL

Sharp, ruby-red bitter spirits that pep up cocktails like the New Classico Spritz and form the basis of the Negroni and Americano. They are really quite life-changing when mixed with soda water and chilled sparkling wine.

TEQUILA

The agave-based brain melter. Unaged (or aged for no more than 60 days in steel containers), silver (*blanco*) tequila is an essential part of your back bar. Gold tequila is sweet and smooth, coloured and flavoured with caramel; *reposado* (rested) tequila, aged in wood-lined tanks or barrels, brings a smoky undertone to your mixes.

VERMOUTH

The fortified wine packed with botanicals, in sweet or dry versions. Get both and keep them refrigerated after opening.

MIXERS

They say no one uses cola as a mixer any more. No one. (Although you're permitted a splash in a Long Island Iced Tea.) But it seems the vodka and cola is the drink that'll never die. Make sure you have the odd can to hand, and keep ginger beer or ale, sparkling water, prosecco, cava or Champagne, freshly-squeezed citrus juices, coconut water and – always – a truckload of ice in stock.

RUM

White, gold, spiced: molasses- or sugarcane-spirit rum is the hoary old sailor's go-to spirit, aged in oak barrels for a woody, put-hair-on-your-chest taste.

WHISKY

For mixing, pick a sturdy, deep-tasting bourbon rather than an aged malt. Monkey Shoulder, Knob Creek and Bulleit Bourbon are all strong contenders.

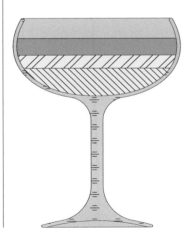

Infusions, Syrups, Brines and Sours: How to Make Your Own

VODKA SOAKS UP ALL MANNER OF FLAVOURS, CREATING A SMOOTH SIPPER OR COCKTAIL MUST-HAVE. CREATE YOUR OWN HEADY BREW OR TRY THESE DELICIOUS RECIPES OUT FOR SIZE.

INFUSIONS

SPICED VODKA

INGREDIENTS

1 whole vanilla pod (bean)
500 ml (17 oz) good vodka
pinch of cardamom pods
4–5 cloves
1 cinnamon stick
palm-size piece of orange peel
(100% pith free)
1 liquorice root stick
thumb-sized piece of peeled
ginger

METHOD Cut the vanilla pod lengthways before adding to the vodka and gently crush the cardamom pods – they'll split open so the seeds can fall out. The cloves and cinnamon lend a warming, exotic note and the orange peel aroma is particularly uplifting (although use sparingly as its flavour is notoriously bitter. Make sure you've trimmed away all the white pith). The liquorice root should add a little sweetness, while the fresh ginger adds a fresh, verdant zing. Steep the ingredients in the vodka in a sterilised bottle (or use the vodka bottle itself, pouring out a little before infusing to make room for the ingredients). Leave in a dark, cool place for at least 2 days – or longer if you want a stronger taste. Strain the ingredients from the liquid and serve.

GINGER VODKA

INGREDIENTS

thumb-sized piece of peeled
ginger
juice of ½ lemon
1 tbsp dark muscovado sugar
500 ml (17 oz) good vodka

METHOD

Steep the ingredients in the vodka and leave for at least 3 days in a cool, dark place straining and refrigerating. Serve when it takes your fancy.

HONEY PEPPER VODKA

INGREDIENTS

1 tbsp freshly ground black pepper
2 tbsp runny honey
500 ml (17 oz) good vodka

METHOD Steep the ingredients in the vodka in a dark, cool place for at least 2 days – or longer if you want a stronger taste. Strain the ingredients from the liquid if you fancy, or leave in for a peppery look.

STAR ANISE VODKA

INGREDIENTS

1–2 star anise pods
1 cinnamon stick
1 tbsp light brown sugar
500 ml (17 oz) good vodka

METHOD

Steep the ingredients in the vodka for at least 3 days in a cool, dark place before straining and serving. before straining and serving.

BAY LEAF VODKA

INGREDIENTS

2–3 fresh (not dried) bay leaves
500 ml (17 oz) good vodka

METHOD

Steep the bay leaves in the vodka and let it steep for at least 3 days in a cool, dark place before straining and serving.

CINNAMON COFFEE VODKA

INGREDIENTS

500 ml (17 oz) good vodka
2 cinnamon sticks
2 shots of fresh espresso, cooled
1 tbsp dark muscovado sugar

METHOD Steep the ingredients in the vodka in a dark, cool place for 2 days – or longer if you want a stronger taste. Perfect for Espresso Martinis or as a sweet sipper.

SYRUPS

The sweet stuff. Taking the edge off sour citrus flavours and softening the taste of bitter spirits, a dash of sugar syrup can transform a drink, turning the toughest liquor into soda pop. Flavoured syrup adds a level of complexity a fresh ingredient just can't achieve. And it's very nearly foolproof to make – start with the Simple Syrup recipe below, graduate to the flavoured recipes, and then begin to create your own. You could always buy them ready-made, but they're so simple, so you really don't need to.

It's not essential to use unrefined sugar, but it's tastier, chemical-free and – used in all your cocktail recipes and syrup-making – lends a wobbly irregularity to proceedings that could only be handmade.

SIMPLE SYRUP

Makes enough dashes for
approximately 15 drinks

INGREDIENTS

200 ml (7 oz) water
100 g (3½ oz) demerara, cane
or granulated sugar
1 tbsp golden syrup or corn syrup
(optional)

EQUIPMENT Non-stick
saucepan, wooden spoon, 200 ml
(7 oz) Kilner (Mason) jar or glass
bottle with stopper and a funnel

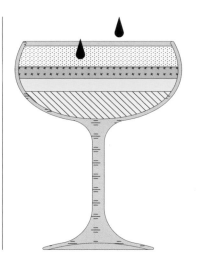

METHOD Boil the water in a non-stick saucepan and gently add the sugar. Reduce the heat and stir constantly with a wooden spoon for 3–5 minutes, until all the sugar is dissolved and the syrup is clear. Turn off the heat and leave to cool. While still runny, pour into a sterilised Kilner (Mason) jar or funnel into a sterilised glass bottle with stopper. Adding a spoonful of golden or corn syrup to the cooled mixture now will help keep the syrup smooth. Store in the refrigerator for up to 6 weeks.

CHERRY AND THYME SYRUP

Makes enough dashes for approximately 15 drinks

INGREDIENTS

200 ml (7 oz) water
100 g (3½ oz) demerara, cane or granulated sugar
handful of ripe, squishy cherries, stoned (pitted)
large sprig of fresh thyme

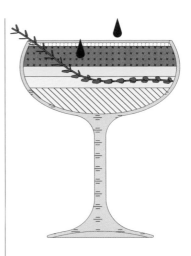

1 tbsp golden syrup or corn syrup (optional)

EQUIPMENT Non-stick saucepan, wooden spoon, 200 ml (7 oz) Kilner (Mason) jar or glass bottle with stopper and a funnel

METHOD Boil the water in a non-stick saucepan and gently add the sugar, cherries and thyme. Reduce the heat and stir constantly for 3–5 minutes, until all the sugar is dissolved. Turn off the heat and leave to cool. While still runny, pour into a sterilised Kilner (Mason) jar or funnel into a sterilised glass bottle with stopper. Adding a spoonful of golden or corn syrup to the cooled mixture will help keep the syrup smooth. Store in the refrigerator for up to 6 weeks.

PINE TIP SYRUP

Makes enough dashes for approximately 15 drinks

INGREDIENTS

200 ml (7 oz) water
100 g (3½ oz) demerara, cane or granulated sugar
handful of freshly picked pine tips (the little bright green leaves from spruce or pine trees)
1 tbsp golden syrup or corn syrup (optional)

EQUIPMENT Non-stick saucepan, wooden spoon, 200 ml (7 oz) Kilner (Mason) jar or glass bottle with stopper and a funnel

METHOD Boil the water in a non-stick saucepan and gently add the sugar and pine tips. Reduce the heat and stir constantly with a wooden spoon for 3–5 minutes, until all the sugar is dissolved and the syrup is clear. Turn off the heat and leave to cool. While still runny, pour into a sterilised Kilner (Mason) jar or funnel into a sterilised glass bottle with stopper. Adding a spoonful of golden or corn syrup to the cooled mixture will help keep the syrup smooth. Store in the refrigerator for up to 6 weeks.

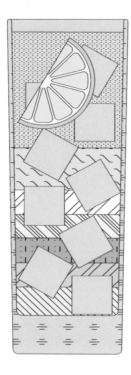

SWEET AND SOUR MIX

Sweet & Sour is the name given to the perfect balance of sugar syrup and fresh citrus juice (it's equal parts Simple Syrup and citrus juice) that can be made ahead of time or created in small amounts per drink.

OTHER INFUSED SYRUPS

Using Simple Syrup (page 37) as the base, make your own infusions, tweaking amounts to taste according to the potency of your flavourings. A sprig or two for rosemary syrup should do it, whereas mint or basil syrups – with the leaves being more fragile – require a good handful. It's not an exact science. Oh, and be sparing with citrus peel as it tends to become bitter.

Basil and Lime
Black Pepper
Chilli
Ginger
Ground Coffee
Honey
Mint
Rosemary
Vanilla Pod (Bean)

SOURS

Sours – a citrus-based mix that can (but not always) include sugar syrup and egg white or aquafaba (tinned chickpea (garbanzo bean) water) – are used to cut through the gloopy sweetness of liqueurs. Shaken up with sugar syrup, a hit of fresh lemon and lime juice, or grapefruit and blood orange, is the fizzing top note of recipes like the classic Whisky or Boston Sour. But a simple half-measure of lemon juice and sugar syrup stirred through a glass of premium vodka on the rocks will also do the trick, turning a fiery sipper into sweetness.

SIMPLE SOUR MIX

INGREDIENTS

15 ml (½ oz) lemon juice, freshly squeezed
15 ml (½ oz) lime juice, freshly squeezed

METHOD Mix both juices and deploy.

CLASSIC SOUR MIX

INGREDIENTS

15 ml (½ oz) lemon juice, freshly squeezed
15 ml (½ oz) lime juice, freshly squeezed
15 ml (½ oz) Simple Syrup (page 37)
1 egg white or 3 tbsp aquafaba

METHOD Mix both juices, sugar syrup and egg white/aquafaba together and shake over ice with your chosen spirit.

BRINES

Brines: salty infusions stolen from olive, caper and pickle jars add a savoury, acid kick to a drink, cutting through sweetness with more brute strength than citrus. But adding brine to an already hard, sharp liquor almost underlines its power. The best bit? It's like having a drink and dinner in one, which – frankly – allows time for more drinking.

The Recipes

VODKA'S PURE, FRESH TASTE UNDERLINES
THE FLAVOURS OF THESE CLASSIC AND
CONTEMPORARY RECIPES.

THE CLASSICS

AGE-OLD, CLASSIC VODKA CONCOCTIONS TOP
EVERY UPSCALE COCKTAIL LIST, AND SO THEY
SHOULD. PERFECTLY BALANCED, AND EACH
WITH ITS OWN SECRET HISTORY, THESE
VODKA-POWERED RECIPES HIT THE SPOT
IN THE CLASSIEST WAY IMAGINABLE.

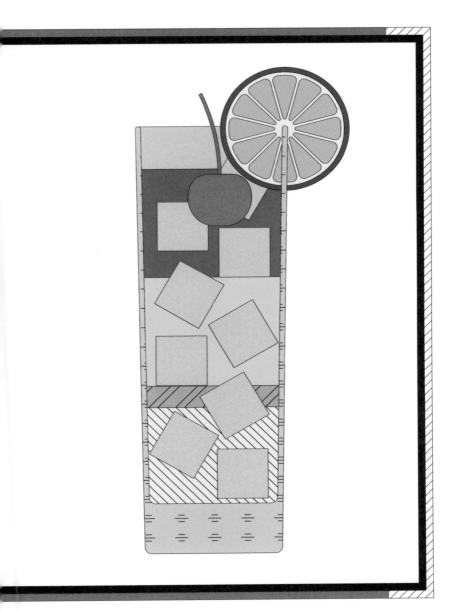

ULTIMATE BLOODY MARY

Everyone has their own version of this classic brunch drink, but this garlic, cucumber and horseradish-infused recipe will win anyone over. Makes 4.

INGREDIENTS

1	tomato juice	1 litre (34 oz/4 cups)
2	vodka	230 ml (8 oz/1 cup)
3	pickle juice	80 ml (3 oz/⅓ cup)
4	Worcestershire sauce	2 tsp
5	hot creamed horseradish	1 tsp
6	garlic, minced	1 clove
7	cucumber, peeled and seeded	1 medium
8	Tabasco	dash
9	freshly ground black pepper	1 tsp
10	sea salt	generous pinch
11	smoked paprika	1 tsp
12	large pickles, cut into spears	to garnish
13	lemon wedges	to garnish

EQUIPMENT Blender

METHOD Blend the ingredients (except the pickle spears and lemon) then pour into Boston or highball glasses half-filled with ice. Add the pickle spears and lemon to garnish.

GLASS TYPE:
BOSTON
OR HIGHBALL

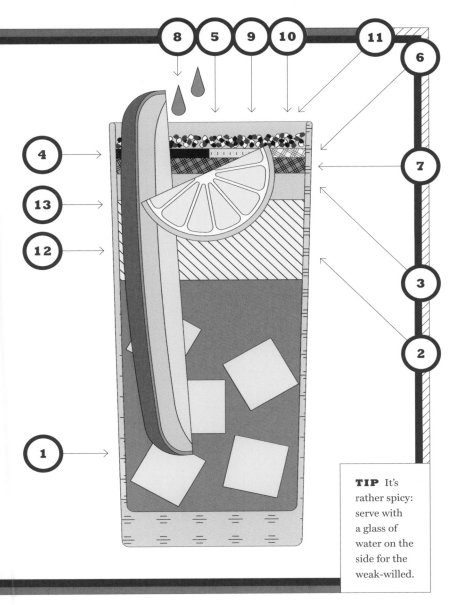

TIP It's rather spicy: serve with a glass of water on the side for the weak-willed.

VODKA COLLINS

This classic cocktail lets the vodka sing. Use a premium spirit, super-fresh lemon juice, and – as this recipe is on the sweet side – feel free to tone down the syrup to taste.

INGREDIENTS

1	premium vodka	60 ml (2 oz)
2	lemon juice, freshly squeezed	30 ml (1 oz)
3	agave or Simple Syrup (page 37)	30 ml (1 oz)
4	chilled soda water	to top up
5	Angostura bitters	2 drops

EQUIPMENT Shaker, strainer

METHOD Shake the vodka, lemon juice and syrup vigorously over ice. Strain into a coupe or flute and top up with chilled soda water. Add a couple of drops of Angostura bitters.

GLASS TYPE
COUPE OR FLUTE

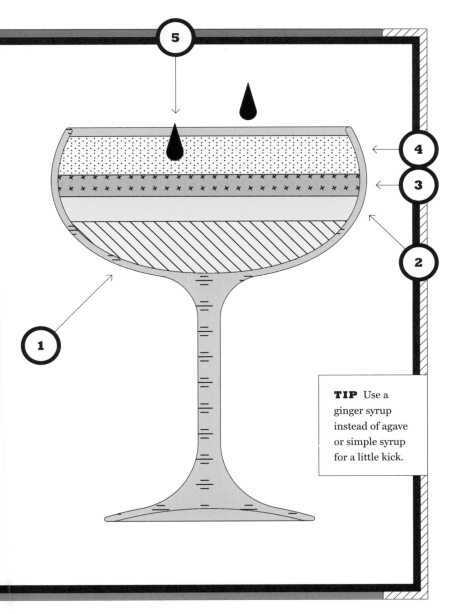

TIP Use a ginger syrup instead of agave or simple syrup for a little kick.

COSMOPOLITAN

The taste of the 90s. This pink, sharp, vodka-based cocktail dominated the upscale drinkeries of New York, London and beyond, getting all manner of bright young hen-nighters tipsy in the process. The Cosmo may have drifted out of the spotlight somewhat, but it's still a classic – and is truly delicious.

INGREDIENTS

1	mandarin or premium vodka	50 ml (1¾ oz)
2	triple sec	25 ml (¾ oz)
3	cranberry juice	25 ml (¾ oz)
4	orange peel	to garnish

EQUIPMENT Shaker, strainer

METHOD Shake the ingredients with ice and strain into a chilled coupe or martini glass. Garnish with orange peel and serve.

GLASS TYPE:
COUPE OR MARTINI

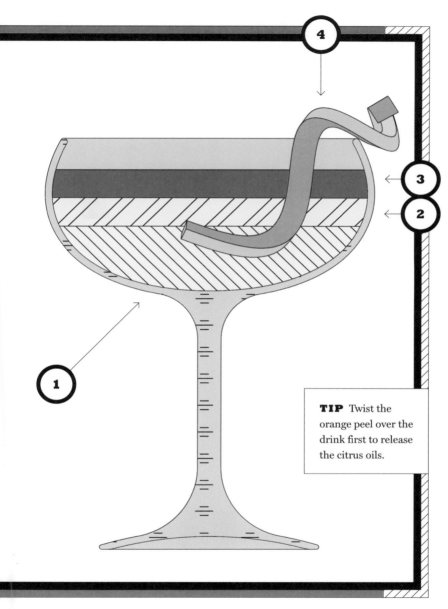

TIP Twist the orange peel over the drink first to release the citrus oils.

SEA BREEZE

Harking from the 1920s, the Sea Breeze has evolved from a simple gin and grenadine cocktail to this juicy and smooth vodka-powered classic.

INGREDIENTS

1	premium vodka	60 ml (2 oz)
2	grapefruit juice, freshly squeezed	150 ml (5 oz)
3	cranberry juice	100 ml (3½ oz)
4	lime juice, freshly squeezed	½ lime
5	lime wheel	to garnish
6	citrus bitters	2 drops

METHOD Add the ingredients to a Boston glass or highball filled with ice in the order above (pour gently to create an ombré effect). Garnish with the lime wheel and top with the bitters.

GLASS TYPE:
BOSTON
OR HIGHBALL

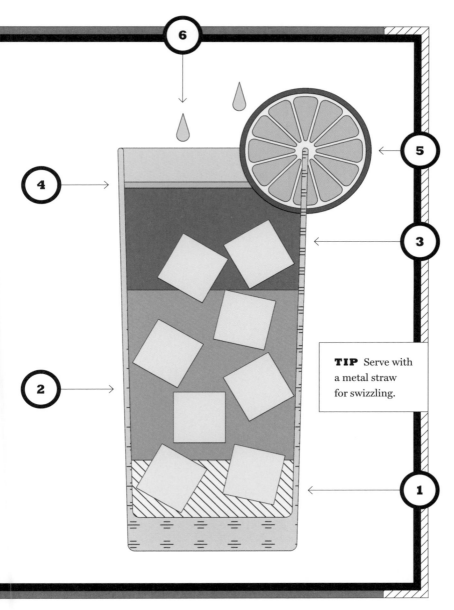

TIP Serve with a metal straw for swizzling.

MOSCOW MULE

The classic vodka cocktail, popular in NYC in the 1940s (and said to be the result of a thrifty bartender's excess stock clear-out) remains one of the finest ways to drink vodka.

INGREDIENTS

1	{	premium vodka	60 ml (2 oz)
2	{	lime juice, freshly squeezed	½ lime
3	{	agave or Simple Syrup (page 37)	30 ml (1 oz)
4	{	fiery ginger beer	to top up

EQUIPMENT Shaker, strainer

METHOD Shake the vodka, lime and syrup with ice, strain into a chilled Moscow mule mug over ice and top up with ginger beer.

GLASS TYPE:
MOSCOW MULE MUG

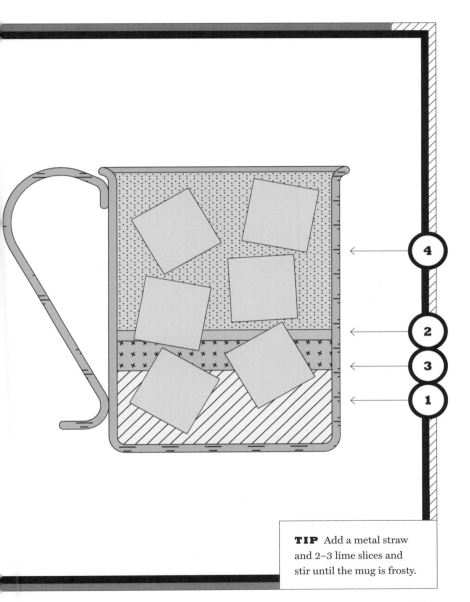

TIP Add a metal straw and 2–3 lime slices and stir until the mug is frosty.

THE REINVENTIONS

CLASSIC VODKA COCKTAILS REWORKED FOR MODERN TIMES. WE'VE RAMMED A PINEAPPLE INTO A MULE AND REWORKED THE CLASSIC SPRITZ. LIKE ALL THE BEST THINGS IN LIFE, ALL YOU NEED IS A LITTLE TWIST.

PINEAPPLE MOSCOW MULE

A pineapple-powered Mule with a tiki twist: a tropical version of the classic 1940s vodka cocktail.

INGREDIENTS

1	premium vodka	60 ml (2 oz)
2	pineapple juice	60 ml (2 oz)
3	lime juice, freshly squeezed	½ lime
4	chilled ginger beer	to top up
5	lime wedges	to garnish

EQUIPMENT Shaker, strainer

METHOD Shake the vodka, pineapple and lime juices with ice, strain into a Moscow mule mug over ice and top up with ginger beer. Garnish with lime wedges.

GLASS TYPE:
MOSCOW MULE
MUG

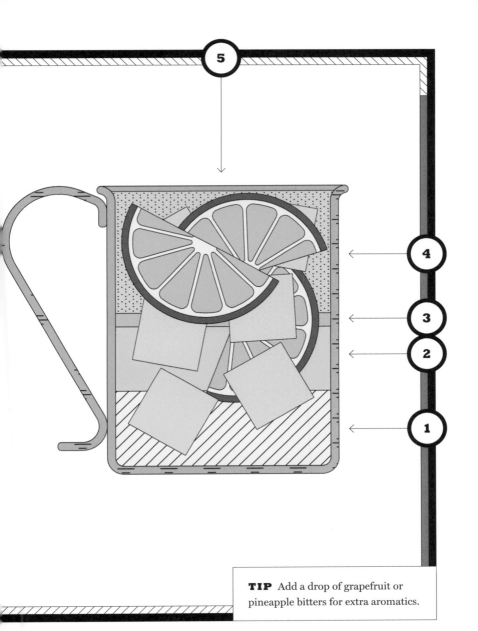

TIP Add a drop of grapefruit or pineapple bitters for extra aromatics.

BEVERLY HILLS ICED TEA

A luxury version of the classic cocktail, swapping the quaint fishing villages of the New York State coastline for the sunshine glamour of Beverly Hills. This version is powered by smooth premium vodka and topped with chilled Champagne.

INGREDIENTS

1	premium vodka	15 ml (½ oz)
2	gold tequila	15 ml (½ oz)
3	gold rum	15 ml (½ oz)
4	gin	15 ml (½ oz)
5	triple sec	15 ml (½ oz)
6	Sweet and Sour Mix (page 40)	30 ml (1 oz)
7	chilled Champagne	to top up
8	lemon wedge	to garnish

EQUIPMENT Shaker, strainer

METHOD Pour all of the ingredients (except the Champagne and lemon wedge) into a shaker filled with ice. Shake until cold and frothy, then strain into a chilled collins glass filled with ice. Top up with Champagne and squeeze a lemon wedge on top.

GLASS TYPE:
COLLINS

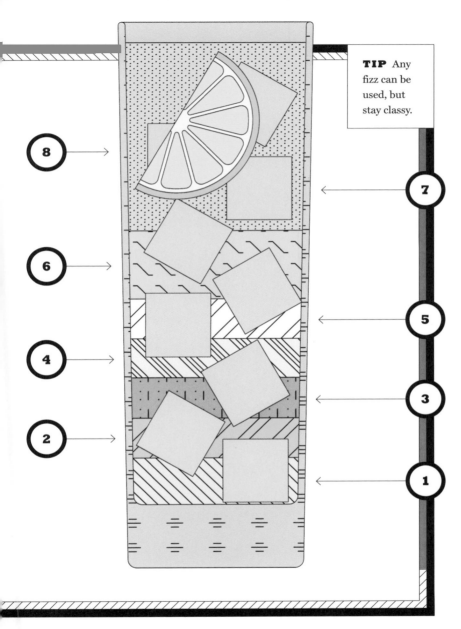

TIP Any fizz can be used, but stay classy.

RASPBERRY COSMOPOLITAN

A contemporary version that blows a raspberry at the pink, sharp, vodka-based cocktail that dominated 90s cocktail culture. It's a shade sweeter than the classic Cosmo, but remains dry enough for the cocktail purists.

INGREDIENTS

1	Absolut Citron vodka	50 ml (1¾ oz)
2	triple sec	15 ml (½ oz)
3	crème de raspberry	15 ml (½ oz)
4	cranberry juice	25 ml (¾ oz)
5	raspberry	to garnish

EQUIPMENT Shaker, strainer

METHOD Shake the liquids with ice and strain into a chilled martini glass or coupe. Garnish with a raspberry and serve.

GLASS TYPE:
MARTINI OR COUPE

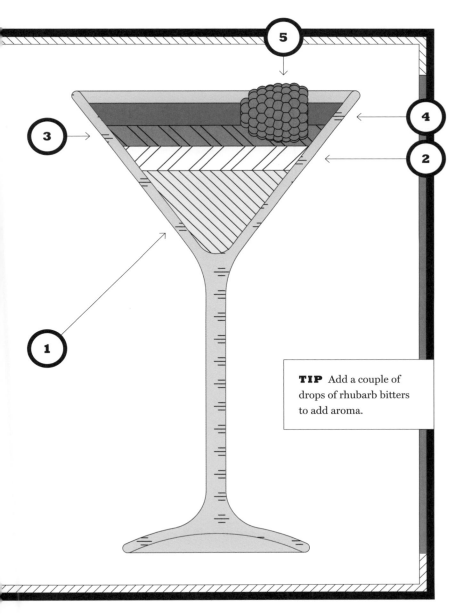

TIP Add a couple of drops of rhubarb bitters to add aroma.

NEW CLASSICO SPRITZ

The non-classic take on the traditional Spritz that's becoming a classic in its own right. Try using Contratto Bitter in favour of Campari or Aperol (although all three work beautifully) and get used to your new default summer drink.

INGREDIENTS

1	vodka	30 ml (1 oz)
2	Aperol or other bitter liqueur	30 ml (1 oz)
3	St-Germain elderflower liqueur	15 ml (½ oz)
4	grapefruit juice, freshly squeezed	25 ml (¾ oz)
5	chilled prosecco	to top up

METHOD Add vodka, Aperol, elderflower liqueur and grapefruit juice to a glass over ice, top up with chilled prosecco and serve with a straw.

GLASS TYPE: WINE, TUMBLER OR HIGHBALL

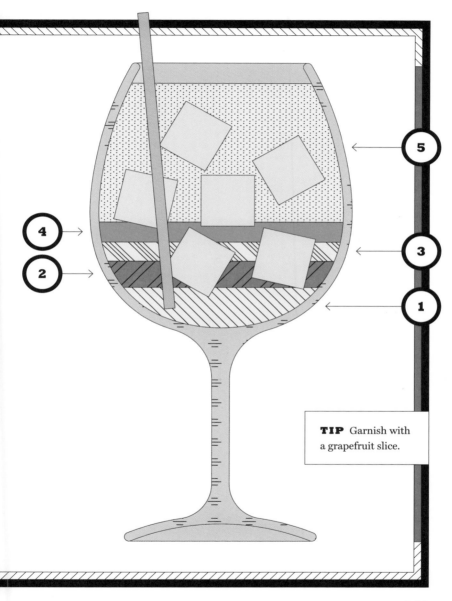

TIP Garnish with a grapefruit slice.

THE
CITRUS-POWERED

VODKA AND CITRUS: THE FINEST BEDFELLOWS.
FRESH SQUEEZINGS OF LIME, LEMON AND
GRAPEFRUIT AND PUNGENT PEEL GARNISHES
ELEVATE THE SPIRIT TO AN OTHERWORLDLY
LEVEL. FROM THE DELICATELY SHARP
GRAPEFRUIT RIVERA TO THE PEPPER POT.

GRAPEFRUIT RIVERA

Lightly bitter grapefruit balanced with sweet and fragrant elderflower, underpinned with a power-punch of premium vodka. A fragile-looking concoction that hides a real strength.

INGREDIENTS

1	premium vodka	60 ml (2 oz)
2	St-Germain elderflower liqueur	30 ml (1 oz)
3	pink grapefruit juice, freshly squeezed	50 ml (1¾ oz)

EQUIPMENT Shaker, strainer

METHOD Shake all the ingredients with ice until frosty and strain into a chilled coupe or martini glass.

GLASS TYPE:
COUPE OR MARTINI

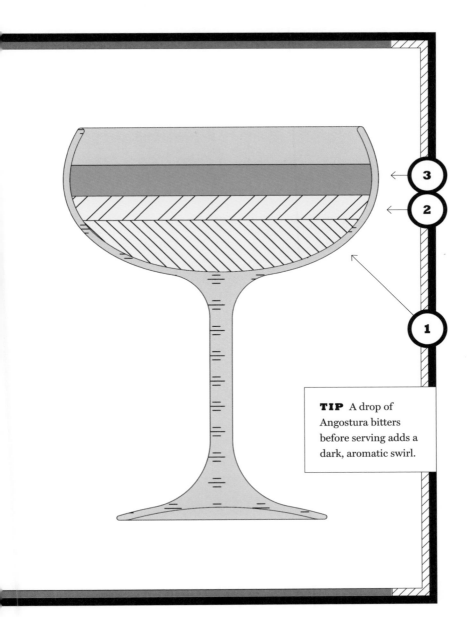

TIP A drop of Angostura bitters before serving adds a dark, aromatic swirl.

PINK PALOMA

This fresh, zingy drink, topped with chilled soda water, uses mandarin or premium vodka as its base, pepped up with ruby grapefruit and lime. The original Paloma, with tequila and a splash of grapefruit soda, is popular in Spain, but this grown-up vodka version of the Spanish teen fave is just the ticket.

INGREDIENTS

1	mandarin or premium vodka	60 ml (2 oz)
2	ruby grapefruit, freshly squeezed	½ grapefruit
3	lime juice, freshly squeezed	15 ml (½ oz)
4	agave or Simple Syrup (page 37)	15 ml (½ oz)
5	soda water	to top up
6	lime wheel	to garnish

EQUIPMENT Shaker, strainer

METHOD Pour the vodka, juices and syrup into an ice-filled shaker. Shake vigorously and strain into an ice-filled jam jar or tumbler. Top up with soda and garnish with a lime wheel.

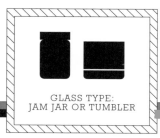

GLASS TYPE:
JAM JAR OR TUMBLER

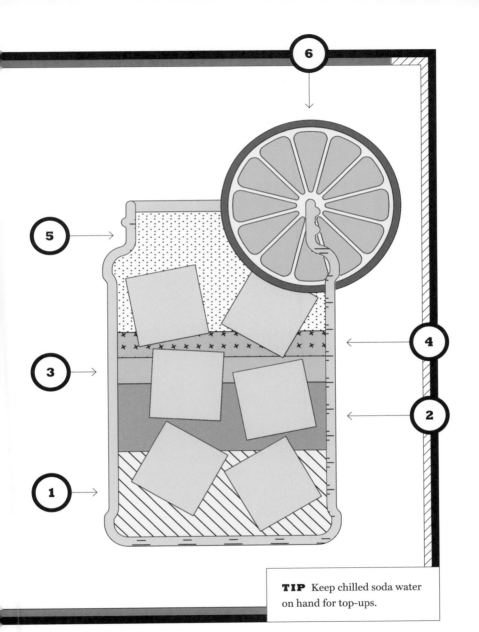

TIP Keep chilled soda water on hand for top-ups.

THE PEPPER POT

The Pepper Pot is a fiery little number: a short, opaque and fruity sipper with warm, spicy notes and a sharp citrus tang, which hits the bitter/sweet ratio dead on.

INGREDIENTS

1	premium vodka	45 ml (1½ oz)
2	Black Pepper Syrup (page 40)	45 ml (1½ oz)
3	grapefruit juice, freshly squeezed	90 ml (3 oz)
4	grapefruit peel or wedge	to garnish

EQUIPMENT Shaker, strainer

METHOD Shake the vodka, syrup and grapefruit juice vigorously with ice until frosty and strain into a tumbler over ice. Garnish with a grapefruit peel or wedge.

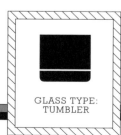

GLASS TYPE:
TUMBLER

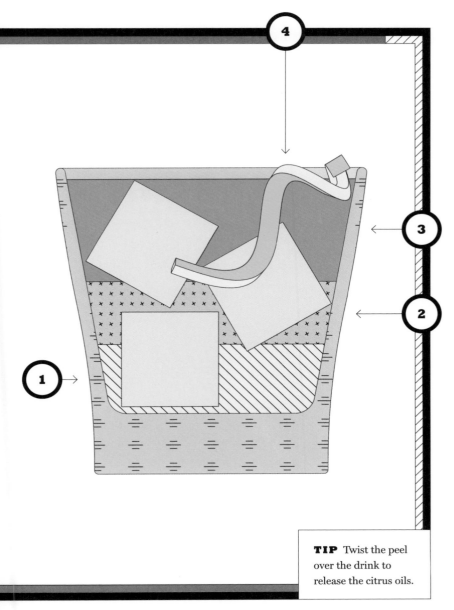

TIP Twist the peel over the drink to release the citrus oils.

KAMIKAZE

The drink medically proven to put hair on your chest. This sour-as-anything mouth-caver, aka the Gimlet's evil twin, is only as delicious as the spirits you use, so be extremely generous. Equal parts premium vodka, Cointreau and freshly-squeezed lime juice: the Kamikaze.

INGREDIENTS

1	premium vodka	30 ml (1 oz)
2	Cointreau	30 ml (1 oz)
3	lime juice, freshly squeezed	30 ml (1 oz)
4	lime wheel	to garnish

EQUIPMENT Shaker, strainer

METHOD Shake the vodka, Cointreau and lime juice vigorously with ice until frosty and strain into a martini glass or coupe. Garnish with a lime wheel.

GLASS TYPE:
MARTINI OR COUPE

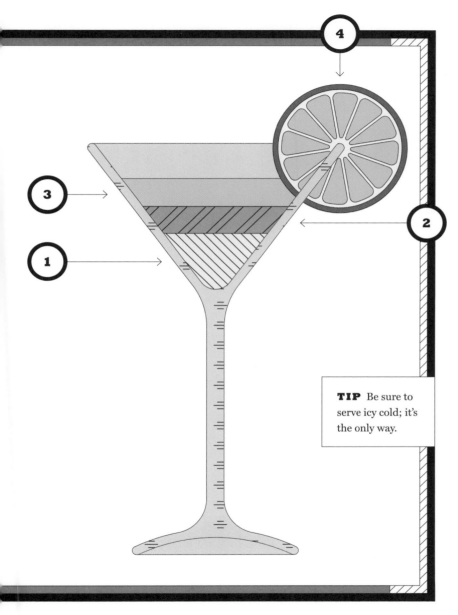

TIP Be sure to serve icy cold; it's the only way.

SEX ON THE BEACH

Because, why not? This cocktail classic may have the most cringe-inducing name in the cocktail world, but it's supremely delicious. Slip on your SPF and enjoy sex on the beach, but without the sand in your gusset.

INGREDIENTS

1	vodka	45 ml (1½ oz)
2	peach liqueur	15 ml (½ oz)
3	smooth orange juice	60 ml (2 oz)
4	cranberry juice	60 ml (2 oz)
5	lime wheel	to garnish
6	glacé cherry	to garnish

METHOD Fill a highball glass with ice cubes, add the liquids in the order above (pour gently to create an orange-to-red ombré effect) and top with a lime wheel slice and glacé cherry for a little retro touch.

GLASS TYPE:
HIGHBALL

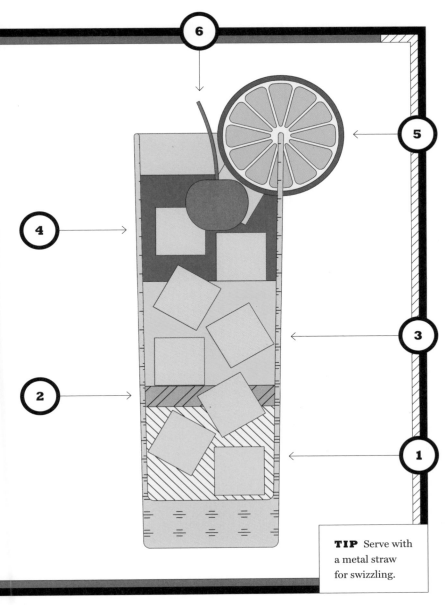

TIP Serve with a metal straw for swizzling.

AFTER DARK

VODKA'S CHAMELEONIC QUALITY MEANS
IT WORKS WONDERFULLY AS AN AFTER-
DINNER DIGESTIF OR AN EYE-CROSSINGLY
POWERFUL LATE-NIGHT PICK-ME-UP.
NO ROOM FOR DESSERT? MIX UP AN
ULTIMATE ESPRESSO MARTINI, GRASSHOPPER
OR MINT STINGER. SWEET AF.

ULTIMATE ESPRESSO MARTINI

This luxury version of the posh party classic uses Patrón's delicious XO Cafe tequila-based liqueur in place of Kahlúa and chocolate bitters for a mind-blowing aroma.

INGREDIENTS

1	premium vodka	60 ml (2 oz)
2	Patrón XO Cafe liqueur	50 ml (1¾ oz)
3	chilled espresso	50 ml (1¾ oz)
4	chocolate bitters	3 drops

EQUIPMENT Shaker, strainer

METHOD Shake the vodka, Patrón and espresso over ice, strain into a chilled martini glass or coupe and top with chocolate bitters.

GLASS TYPE:
MARTINI OR COUPE

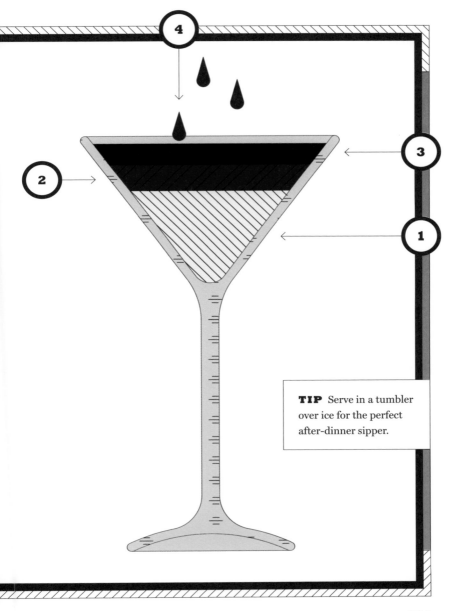

TIP Serve in a tumbler over ice for the perfect after-dinner sipper.

GRASSHOPPER

The classic mint-chocolate cream dessert drink favoured by Halloween party guests and drag queens (after the Daiquiris are drunk dry). The originator of this delicious Muppet-green cocktail is thought to be Philip Guichet of Tujague's bar in New Orleans in 1918. We salute you, sir.

INGREDIENTS

1	vodka	25 ml (¾ oz)
2	fresh cream	25 ml (¾ oz)
3	crème de menthe	15 ml (½ oz)
4	white crème de cacao	15 ml (½ oz)
5	grated chocolate	to garnish

METHOD Shake the liquids over ice and strain into a martini glass or coupe. Garnish with a little grated chocolate.

GLASS TYPE:
MARTINI OR COUPE

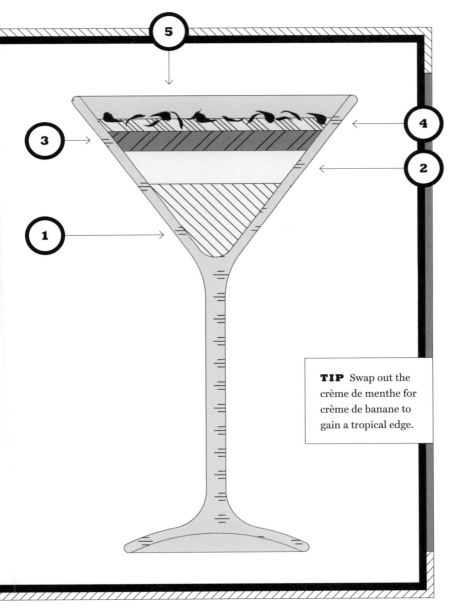

TIP Swap out the crème de menthe for crème de banane to gain a tropical edge.

THE LOCUST

The cream-free, tough-ass cousin of the Grasshopper, this mint-chocolate, emerald green after-dinner drink is perfect for your more entitled, privileged guests, for whom the only thing they can't have in this life is dairy.

INGREDIENTS

1	vodka	25 ml (¾ oz)
2	crème de menthe	25 ml (¾ oz)
3	white crème de cacao	25 ml (¾ oz)

EQUIPMENT Shaker, strainer

METHOD Shake the ingredients over ice until frosty and strain into a coupe or martini glass.

GLASS TYPE:
COUPE OR MARTINI

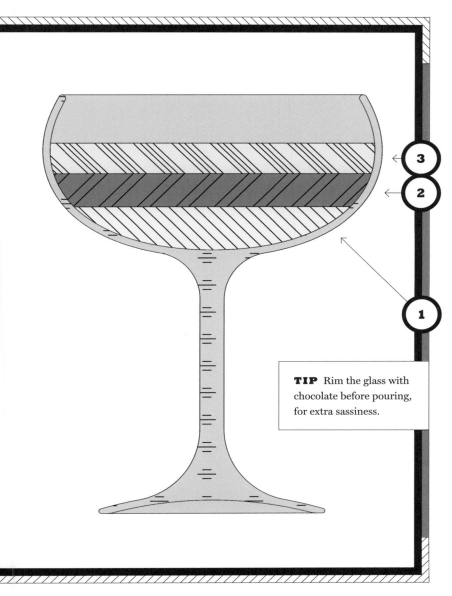

TIP Rim the glass with chocolate before pouring, for extra sassiness.

MINT STINGER

Chocolate and mint: the finest bedfellows. This Vodka Stinger uses mint and chocolate spirits for a sturdy, clear cocktail that looks just like a classic Martini – but isn't.

INGREDIENTS

1	}	premium vodka	60 ml (2 oz)
2	}	white crème de menthe	50 ml (1¾ oz)
3	}	white crème de cacao	50 ml (1¾ oz)
4	}	mint sprig	to garnish

EQUIPMENT Shaker, strainer

METHOD Shake the liquids over ice and strain into a chilled martini glass or coupe. Garnish with a mint sprig.

GLASS TYPE:
MARTINI OR COUPE

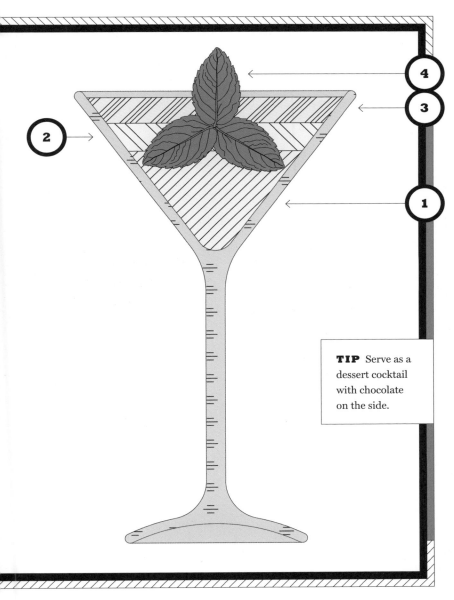

TIP Serve as a dessert cocktail with chocolate on the side.

THE MARTINIS

PURE, SUPER-CHILLED AND MILDLY DEADLY.
THE MARTINI IN ALL ITS CLASSIC
AND FRUITY VERSIONS SHOWCASES THE QUALITY
OF THE SPIRIT: MAKE SURE YOUR VODKA
IS AS FANCY AS POSSIBLE.

APPLETINI

This fresh-tasting Apple Martini straddles the sour/sweet divide with perfect balance. Use a good-quality cloudy apple juice or a clear one for a less homespun-looking drink.

INGREDIENTS

1	premium vodka	60 ml (2 oz)
2	apple liqueur	40 ml (1½ oz)
3	lemon juice, freshly squeezed	30 ml (1 oz)
4	cloudy apple juice	15 ml (½ oz)
5	ginger bitters	2 drops

EQUIPMENT Shaker, strainer

METHOD Shake the vodka, apple liqueur, lemon and apple juices vigorously over ice. Strain into a martini glass or coupe and top with a couple of drops of ginger bitters.

GLASS TYPE:
MARTINI OR COUPE

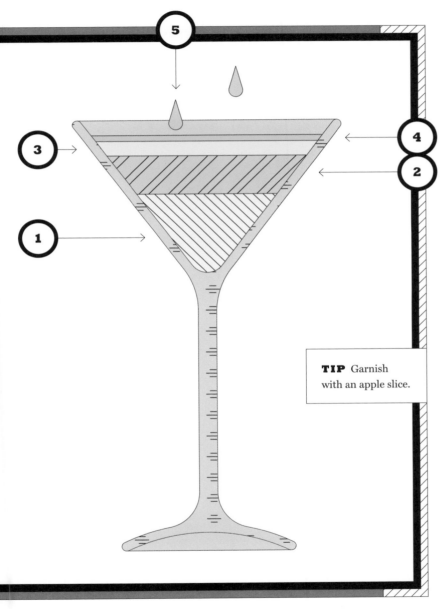

TIP Garnish with an apple slice.

THE VODKA MARTINI

The ultimate classic cocktail, the Vodka Martini consists of just two ingredients: vodka and vermouth, and is fragranced by a lemon twist. Sometimes stirred in a mixing glass, using the shaker adds a frostiness that numbs any sharpness, making it silky smooth. If someone tells you one can't serve a Martini without gin, cut them out of your life.

INGREDIENTS

1	premium vodka	60 ml (2 oz)
2	dry vermouth	15 ml (½ oz)
3	lemon twist	to garnish

EQUIPMENT Shaker, strainer

METHOD Shake the liquids over ice until frosty and slightly diluted (about 20–30 seconds), then strain into a martini glass or coupe. Garnish with a lemon twist.

GLASS TYPE:
MARTINI OR COUPE

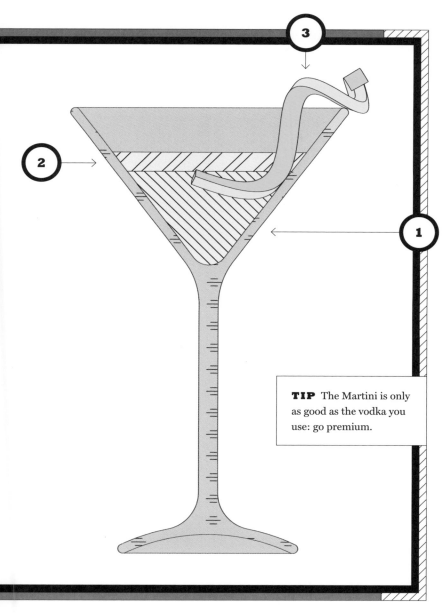

TIP The Martini is only as good as the vodka you use: go premium.

TEENY MARTINI

The pre-mixed, make-ahead version of the classic cocktail, this mini vodka-gin Martini has a soft briny taste with the zing of citrus and fennel. Add the ingredients to a Kilner (Mason) bottle and store in the refrigerator. Best for Martini lovers with a low alcohol threshold. Also perfect for unexpected guests.

INGREDIENTS

1	{	premium vodka	420 ml (14½ oz/1¾ cups)
2	{	gin	420 ml (14½ oz/1¾ cups)
3	{	dry vermouth	140 ml (5 oz/⅔ cup)
4	{	olive or caper berry brine	70 ml (2 ⅓ oz)
5	{	fennel bitters	10 drops
6	{	olive or caper berry	to garnish

EQUIPMENT 1 litre (34 oz) clip-top Kilner (Mason) bottle, shaker, strainer

METHOD Add the liquids to a bottle and store in the refrigerator. Transfer to the freezer about 40 minutes before serving for a super-chilled drink, or freshen up quickly by shaking vigorously over ice before pouring. Serve in a glass with an olive or caper berry to garnish.

GLASS TYPE: SHOT GLASS, MINI MARTINI OR MINI COUPE

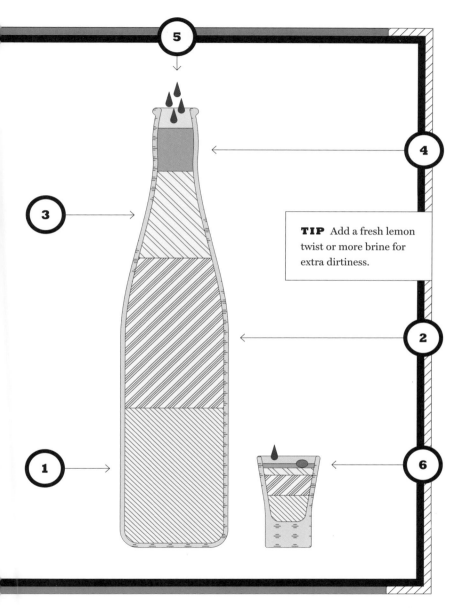

TIP Add a fresh lemon twist or more brine for extra dirtiness.

ESPRESSO MARTINI

AKA gal's rocket fuel. This classic cocktail is the night-time pick-me-up for those who claim they have pilates in the morning and need to retire early. Serve them an Espresso Martini after dinner and watch them tap dance on your coffee table until the early hours.

INGREDIENTS

1	premium vodka	60 ml (2 oz)
2	Kahlúa coffee liqueur	50 ml (1¾ oz)
3	chilled espresso	50 ml (1¾ oz)
4	coffee beans	to garnish

EQUIPMENT Shaker, strainer

METHOD Shake the liquids over ice and strain into a chilled martini glass or coupe. Garnish with 2–3 coffee beans.

GLASS TYPE:
MARTINI OR COUPE

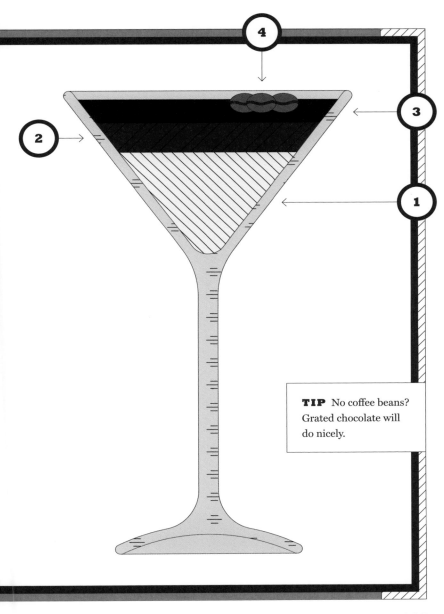

TIP No coffee beans? Grated chocolate will do nicely.

FRENCH MARTINI

The silky, sweet and berry-infused French Martini is a classic. Use Chambord for an authentic taste, fresh or premium pineapple juice, and shake well to create a plump foam top. Swap out the premium vodka for vanilla vodka for extra Frenchiness.

INGREDIENTS

1	premium vodka	30 ml (1 oz)
2	Chambord	30 ml (1 oz)
3	pineapple juice	30 ml (1 oz)

EQUIPMENT Shaker, strainer

METHOD Shake all the ingredients vigorously over ice and strain into a martini glass or coupe.

GLASS TYPE:
MARTINI OR COUPE

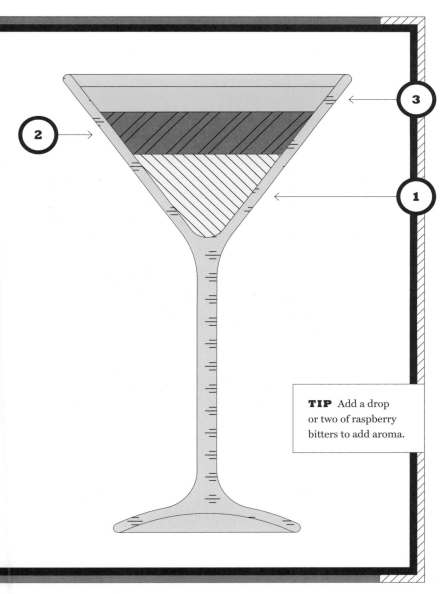

TIP Add a drop or two of raspberry bitters to add aroma.

LONG, LONG DRINKS

FOR THOSE WHO NEVER WANT IT TO END: THESE DELICIOUS PUNCH-LIKE LONG DRINKS QUENCH THIRST AND HIDE VODKA'S FIRE POWER.

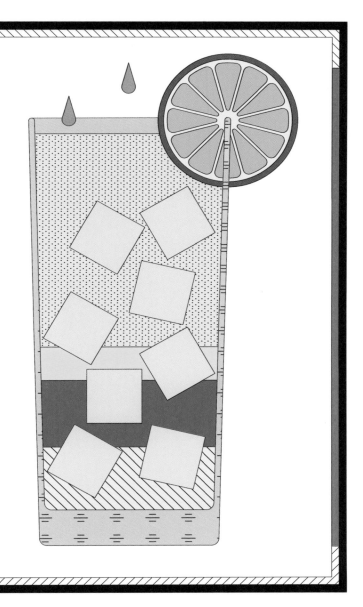

VODKA BASIL SODA

An eye-crossingly refreshing and aromatic long drink, starring your favourite vanilla vodka, elderflower and herbaceous basil, with a grown up, dry taste. It could only be made more delicious with a huge cucumber garnish: what's stopping you?

INGREDIENTS

1	vanilla vodka	30 ml (1 oz)
2	St-Germain elderflower liqueur	15 ml (½ oz)
3	lemon juice, freshly squeezed	dash
4	basil leaves	4–5
5	chilled soda water	to top up

METHOD Add the vodka, elderflower liqueur and lemon juice to a highball glass or tumbler filled halfway with ice. Gently bruise the basil leaves by rolling in your hands and add to the glass, topping up with soda water.

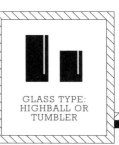

GLASS TYPE:
HIGHBALL OR
TUMBLER

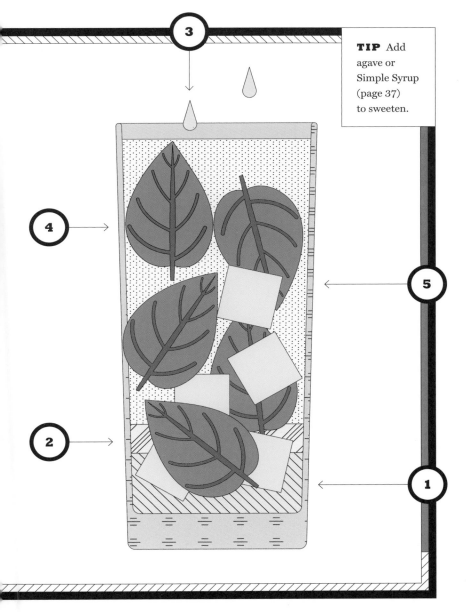

TIP Add agave or Simple Syrup (page 37) to sweeten.

ULTIMATE VODKA ORANGE

Even the most perfect couple needs to open things up once in a while. Change up the classic pairing of vodka and orange with vanilla tones, freshly-squeezed juice and a couple of drops of orange bitters for eye-crossing aromatics. You'll never go back.

INGREDIENTS

1	vanilla vodka	30 ml (1 oz)
2	orange juice, freshly squeezed	to top up
3	orange bitters	2 drops
4	orange wheel	to garnish

METHOD Add the vodka to a highball glass or tumbler filled halfway with ice. Top up with the orange juice and bitters. Garnish with an orange wheel.

GLASS TYPE:
HIGHBALL OR
TUMBLER

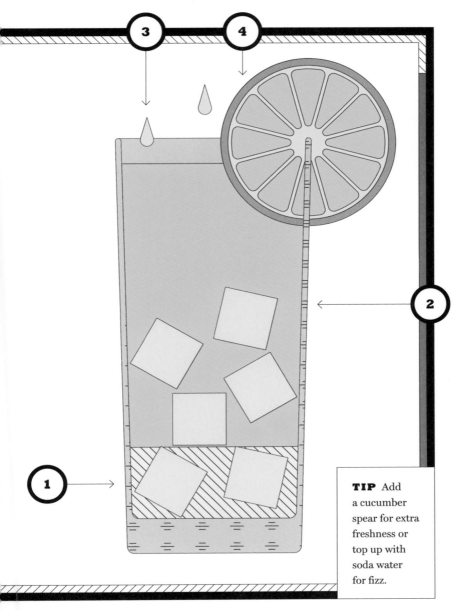

TIP Add a cucumber spear for extra freshness or top up with soda water for fizz.

RUSSIAN SPRING PUNCH

The 1980s in a glass: Russian Spring Punch is up there with the Tequila Sunrise as a drink that embodies a whole decade of classic pop music and dubious haircuts. This highball vodka cocktail is berry-powered with a rather classy Champagne fizz.

INGREDIENTS

1	Absolut Raspberri vodka	30 ml (1 oz)
2	lemon juice, freshly squeezed	30 ml (1 oz)
3	Chambord	10 ml (⅓ oz)
4	agave or Simple Syrup (page 37)	10 ml (⅓ oz)
5	chilled Champagne	to top up
6	mixed berries	to garnish

EQUIPMENT Shaker, strainer

METHOD Shake the ingredients (except for the Champagne and berries) vigorously with ice until frosty and strain into a highball glass over ice. Top up with Champagne and garnish with mixed berries.

GLASS TYPE:
HIGHBALL

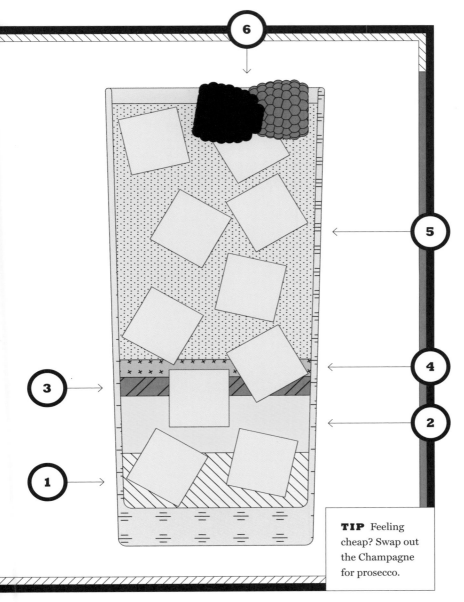

TIP Feeling cheap? Swap out the Champagne for prosecco.

CUCUMBER LEMONADE

Imagine making a fresh, zingy and wholesome lemonade of the type seen at kids' lemonade stands in the 1970s, with a sneaky shot of mum and dad's vodka thrown in, and all the adults get smashed. Keys are thrown in a bowl, and then something happens with a cucumber. That's this drink.

INGREDIENTS

1	vodka		60 ml (2 oz)
2	cucumber juice, freshly squeezed		30 ml (1 oz)
3	lemon juice, freshly squeezed		15 ml (½ oz)
4	agave or Simple Syrup (page 37)		dash
5	chilled soda water		to top up
6	cucumber spear		to garnish

EQUIPMENT Shaker, strainer

METHOD Shake the vodka, cucumber and lemon juices and syrup with ice, then strain and pour into a highball glass full of ice. Top up with chilled soda water and garnish with a cucumber spear.

GLASS TYPE:
HIGHBALL

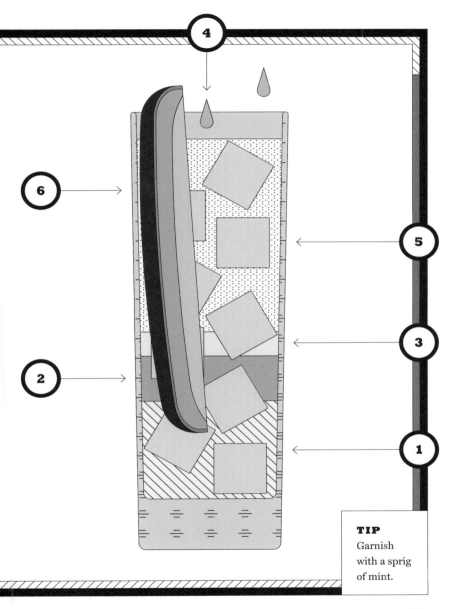

TIP
Garnish
with a sprig
of mint.

POSH BITCH

The classic triumvirate of vodka, lime and soda, aka the Skinny Bitch, is the calorie counter's go-to drink. This version is a little posher, swapping out lime juice for pink grapefruit and is powered by a delicately flavoured mandarin vodka.

INGREDIENTS

1	mandarin vodka	60 ml (2 oz)
2	pink grapefruit juice, freshly squeezed	50 ml (1¾ oz)
3	chilled soda water	to top up

EQUIPMENT Shaker, strainer

METHOD Shake all the ingredients over ice until frosty, then strain into a chilled highball glass and top up with the soda.

GLASS TYPE:
HIGHBALL

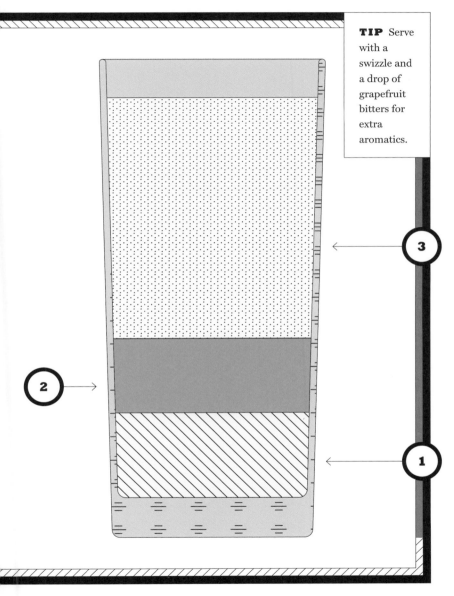

TIP Serve with a swizzle and a drop of grapefruit bitters for extra aromatics.

PINK VODKA LEMONADE

The summer party favourite, Pink Vodka Lemonade is a criminally tasty way to drink vodka. The added lemon juice keeps it tart and the raspberry-infused premium vodka elevates this drink from downgrade party punch to something altogether classier.

INGREDIENTS

1	Absolut Raspberri vodka	30 ml (1 oz)
2	cranberry juice	30 ml (1 oz)
3	lemon juice, freshly squeezed	15 ml (½ oz)
4	chilled lemonade	to top up
5	rhubarb bitters	2 drops
6	lime wheel	to garnish

METHOD Add the vodka, cranberry and lemon juices to a highball glass over ice, then top up with lemonade. Add the bitters and garnish with a lime wheel.

GLASS TYPE:
HIGHBALL

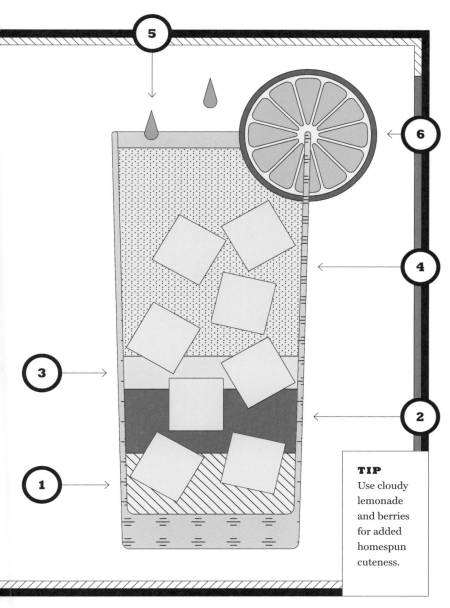

TIP
Use cloudy
lemonade
and berries
for added
homespun
cuteness.

HOUSE PARTY

MAGICAL PARTY-WORTHY CONCOCTIONS THAT CAN BE MADE IN BATCHES, OR WITH A MIND-BENDING TWIST, FROM THE FROZEN COSMO AND LIMONCELLO FLOAT TO A VEGAN-FRIENDLY WHITE RUSSIAN.

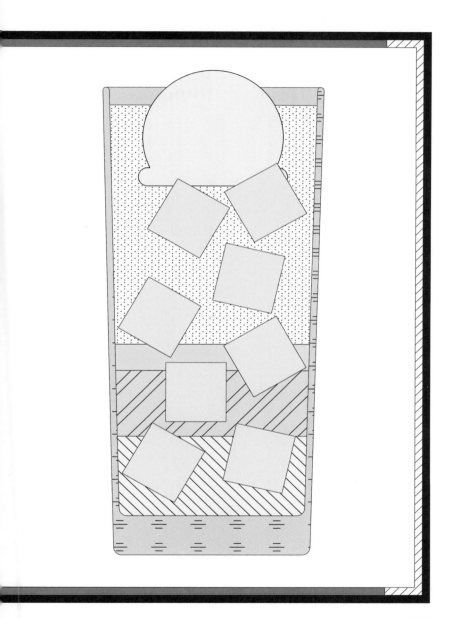

ALMOND WHITE RUSSIAN

This rather attractive, almond-edged White Russian swaps out fresh cream for delicious nut milk and is all the better for it. Make sure your vodka is super-chilled in the freezer and use almond milk straight from the refrigerator. Serve as a dessert (or instead of your morning latte, because why not?).

INGREDIENTS

1	super-chilled vanilla vodka	30 ml (1 oz)
2	Kahlúa coffee liqueur	30 ml (1 oz)
3	chilled almond milk	125 ml (4 oz/½ cup)

METHOD Add the vodka and Kahlúa to a tumbler with a single large ice cube and gently pour over the almond milk to create an ombré effect.

GLASS TYPE:
TUMBLER

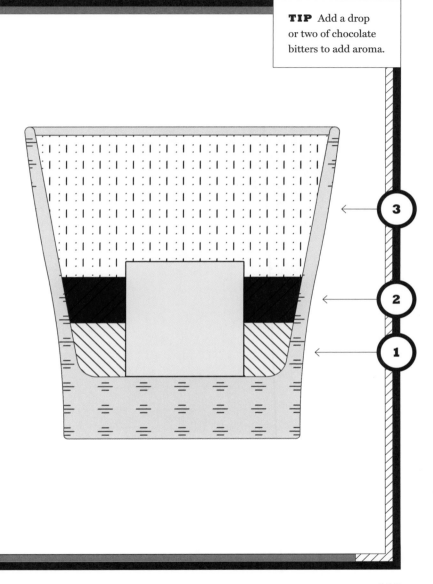

TIP Add a drop or two of chocolate bitters to add aroma.

BLACK MAGIC

Think of this little tasty pick-me-up of a drink as a Black Russian Sour. Vodka, coffee liqueur and lemon juice is an odd three-way, but it somehow works, dammit. Dark arts: mastered.

INGREDIENTS

1	premium vodka	50 ml (1¾ oz)
2	Kahlúa coffee liqueur	50 ml (1¾ oz)
3	lemon juice, freshly squeezed	15 ml (½ oz)

METHOD Add the vodka and Kahlúa to a tumbler with a large ice cube, stir, then drizzle the lemon juice over the top.

GLASS TYPE:
TUMBLER

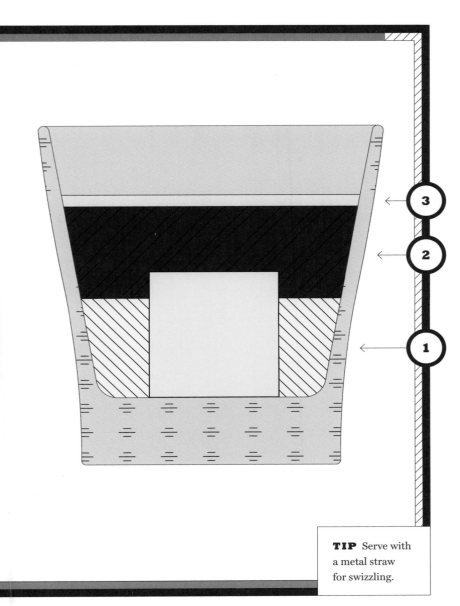

TIP Serve with a metal straw for swizzling.

LIMONCELLO FLOAT

Remember that old adage: when life gives you lemons, you make your own hand-crafted limoncello and citrus sorbet and post about it on Instagram? This lemon-powered drink is a delicious way to show off your handiwork (or just buy in all the ingredients, no one will know) and tastes great, too.

INGREDIENTS

1	premium vodka	30 ml (1 oz)
2	limoncello	30 ml (1 oz)
3	lemon juice, freshly squeezed	15 ml (½ oz)
4	chilled soda water	to top up
5	lemon sorbet	1 tbsp

METHOD Add the vodka, limoncello and lemon juice to a highball glass or tumbler over ice, top up with soda water and stir briefly. Drop in the sorbet scoop and drink as it melts.

GLASS TYPE: HIGHBALL
OR TUMBLER

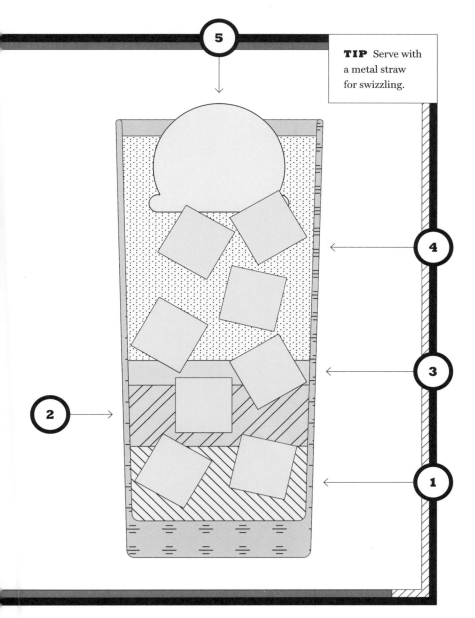

TIP Serve with a metal straw for swizzling.

FROZEN COSMO

Some call the Frozen Cosmo a textural reworking of the classic cranberry cocktail, others call it the gal pal's slushie, but it's delicious whatever you call it. Use a tough-ass blender and crushed (not cubed) ice for a truly silky drink.

INGREDIENTS

1	Absolut Citron vodka	45 ml (1½ oz)
2	Cointreau	15 ml (½ oz)
3	cranberry juice	30 ml (1 oz)
4	lime juice, freshly squeezed	15 ml (½ oz)
5	lime wheel	to garnish

EQUIPMENT Blender

METHOD Add the liquids to a high-power blender with crushed ice and whizz until slushie-like. Pour into a highball, punch glass or bowl and top with a splash more cranberry to loosen, if needed. Garnish with the lime wheel.

GLASS TYPE: HIGHBALL, PUNCH GLASS, PUNCH BOWL OR ANYTHING

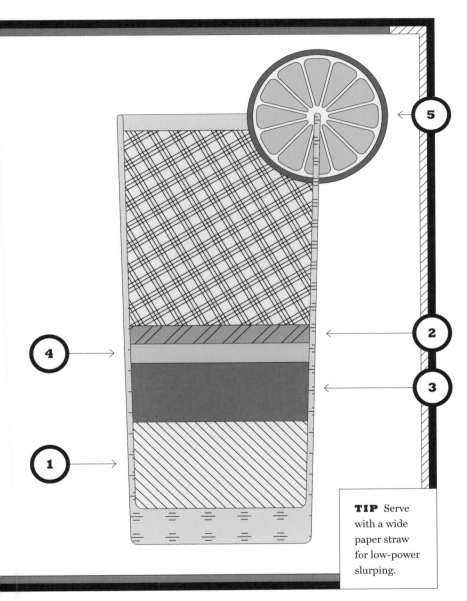

TIP Serve with a wide paper straw for low-power slurping.

HONEY PEPPER PUNCH

Honey pepper vodka is a Ukrainian delicacy and this spicy long drink, topped with premium lager, underlines the flavour of this curious spirit. As with any cocktail that includes lager, don't scrimp and make sure it's premium, light and chilled to perfection.

INGREDIENTS

1	}	honey pepper or premium vodka	30 ml (1 oz)
2	}	Ginger Syrup (page 40)	15 ml (½ oz)
3	}	lime juice, freshly squeezed	10 ml (⅓ oz)
4	}	premium lager	to top up
5	}	lime wheel	to garnish

EQUIPMENT Shaker

METHOD Shake the vodka, syrup and lime juice with ice until frosty. Pour into a highball glass or tumbler over a rock of ice, and top up with premium lager. Garnish with a lime wheel.

GLASS TYPE: HIGHBALL OR TUMBLER

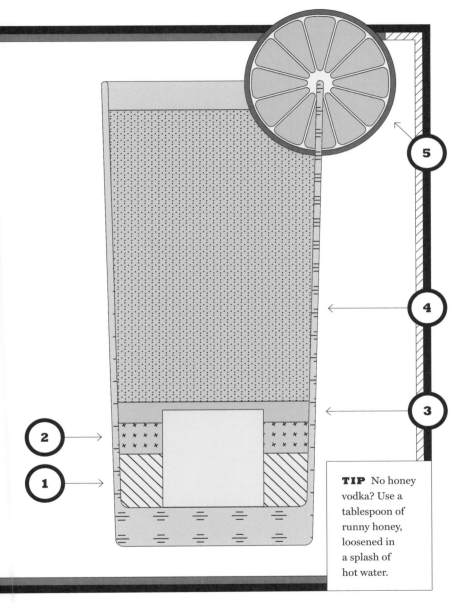

TIP No honey vodka? Use a tablespoon of runny honey, loosened in a splash of hot water.

MODERN CLASSICS

RATHER REFINED, COMPLETELY
CONTEMPORARY: THESE DRINKS SHOW OFF
YOUR HOME MIXING SKILLS WITH RARE
INGREDIENTS, FROM CHARRED LEMONS AND
PINE TIP SYRUP, TO RECIPES WITH REAL
POMEGRANATE POWER.

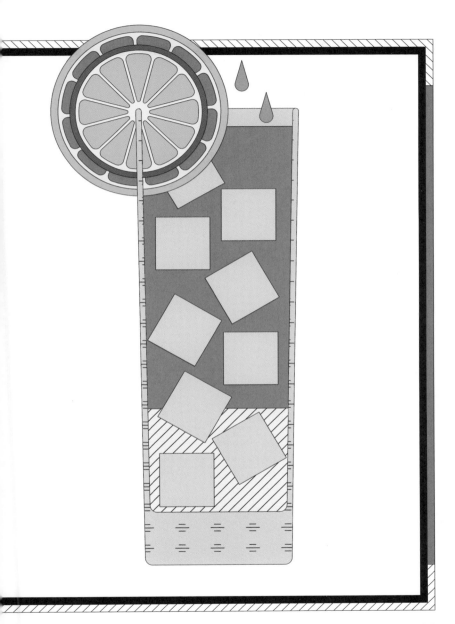

POMEGRANATE SOUR

Pomegranate makes a naturally complex, slightly tart base for this fragrant, tasty recipe. Equal parts premium vanilla vodka and pomegranate juice, plus freshly squeezed lime juice and a dash of ginger syrup, make for a jewel-bright fruity sipper.

INGREDIENTS

1	vanilla vodka	30 ml (1 oz)
2	pomegranate juice	30 ml (1 oz)
3	lime juice, freshly squeezed	15 ml (½ oz)
4	Ginger Syrup (page 40)	15 ml (½ oz)
5	pomegranate seeds	to garnish

EQUIPMENT Shaker, strainer

METHOD Shake the liquids vigorously over ice until frosty and strain into a martini glass or coupe. Garnish with pomegranate seeds.

GLASS TYPE:
MARTINI OR COUPE

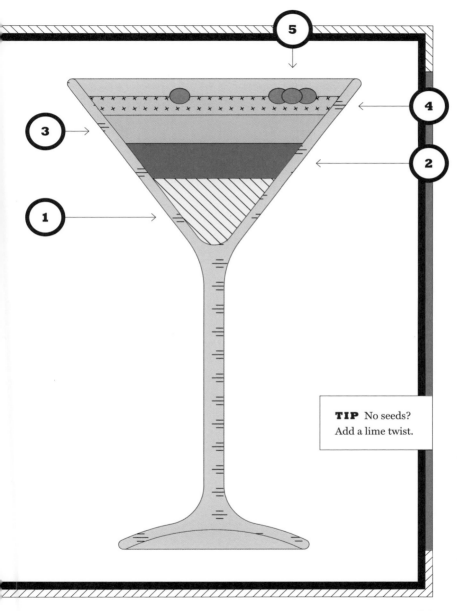

TIP No seeds? Add a lime twist.

CHARRED LEMONADE

This smoky, honey-sweet and fresh citrus long drink is hands-down delicious. Use a premium or a lemon- or mandarin-infused vodka, sweet honey syrup and the freshest, most squidgy lemons you can find.

INGREDIENTS

1	lemons	2–3
2	premium vodka	30 ml (1 oz)
3	Honey Syrup (page 40)	30 ml (1 oz)
4	chilled soda water	to top up
5	thyme sprig	to garnish
6	lemon slices	to garnish

EQUIPMENT Mixing glass, griddle pan

METHOD Halve the lemons and char, flesh-side down, on a hot griddle pan for less than a minute (until lightly charred) then, for the garnish, char a couple of lemon slices for 20 seconds or so. Juice the lemon halves and add 30 ml (1 oz) of the liquid plus the vodka and honey syrup to a mixing glass with ice. Stir until frosty, add to a highball glass and top up with soda. Garnish with a thyme sprig and the charred lemon slices.

GLASS TYPE:
HIGHBALL

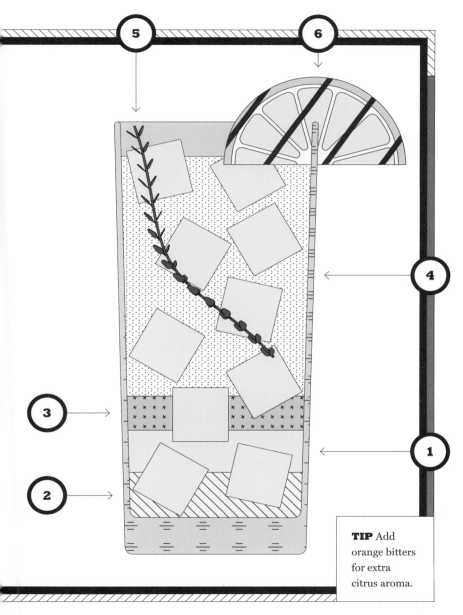

TIP Add
orange bitters
for extra
citrus aroma.

PINE TIP SODA

This woodsy, pine-tip infused sweet soda is a delicious drink. Make your own Pine Tip Syrup (page 40) using bright green new pine tips and let it add a manly, live-in-a-log-cabin vibe to your cocktails. Pine syrup works best in a simple, pared-down recipe, but you can always add a little ginger slice if you're the fancy sort.

INGREDIENTS

1	premium vodka	60 ml (2 oz)
2	Pine Tip Syrup (page 40)	30 ml (1 oz)
3	lemon juice, freshly squeezed	15 ml (½ oz)
4	chilled soda water	to top up

EQUIPMENT Shaker, strainer

METHOD Shake the vodka, syrup and lemon juice over ice until frosty and strain into a coupe. Top up with soda water.

GLASS TYPE:
COUPE

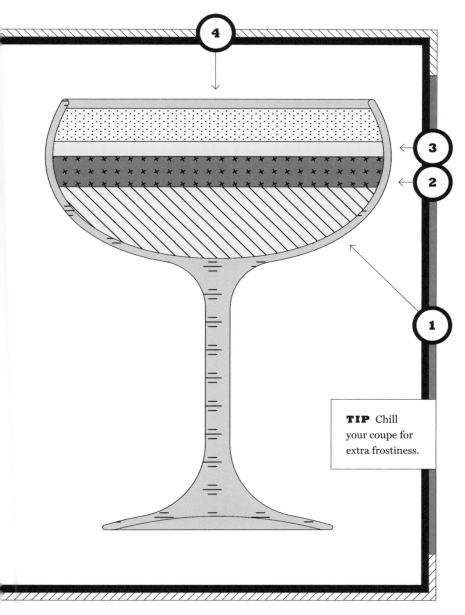

TIP Chill your coupe for extra frostiness.

SOUR CHERRY AND THYME

A dark, rich cherry sour with a soft thyme aroma, edged with sharp, freshly squeezed lime juice. Add the Angostura bitters at the end to cut through the pink-tinged foam.

INGREDIENTS

1	berry vodka	60 ml (2 oz)
2	triple sec	30 ml (1 oz)
3	lime juice, freshly squeezed	30 ml (1 oz)
4	Cherry and Thyme Syrup (page 38)	120 ml (4 oz)
5	egg white (or aquafaba)	1 (or 1 tbsp)
6	thyme sprig	to garnish
7	Angostura bitters	dash

EQUIPMENT Shaker, strainer

METHOD Shake the vodka, triple sec, lime juice, syrup and egg white vigorously over ice. Strain into a coupe, garnish with a sprig of fresh thyme and add a couple of drops of Angostura bitters.

GLASS TYPE:
COUPE

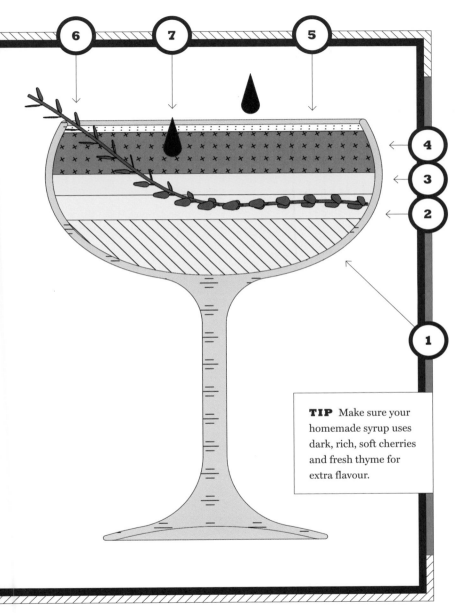

TIP Make sure your homemade syrup uses dark, rich, soft cherries and fresh thyme for extra flavour.

BLOODY SCREWDRIVER

This vodka sipper is a classic, updated with blood orange (rather than orange) for a dark pink hue. If there's a better way to get your daily dose of vitamin C, we'd like to hear it.

INGREDIENTS

1	{	premium vodka	60 ml (2 oz)
2	{	blood orange juice, freshly squeezed	to top up
3	{	lime and blood orange wheels	to garnish
4	{	citrus bitters	2 drops

METHOD Add the vodka and juice to a highball glass or tumbler filled with ice and stir. Add the citrus wheels as a garnish and the bitters to top.

GLASS TYPE: HIGHBALL
OR TUMBLER

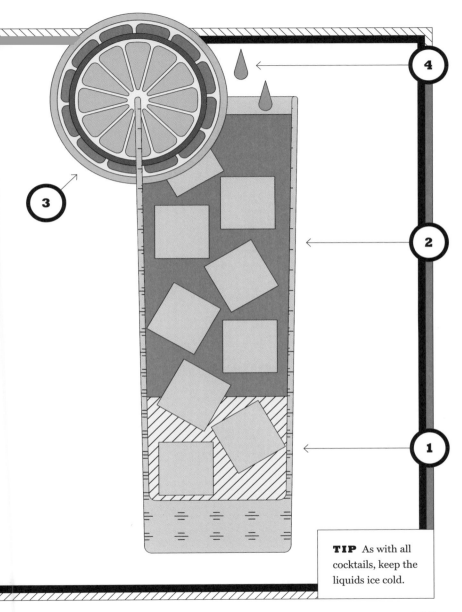

TIP As with all cocktails, keep the liquids ice cold.

POWER SHOT

The ultimate pre-party, going-out drink. This little firecracker has a deceptive sweetness – fresh and zingy with a hot, spicy aftertaste. Also works as a miracle cure-all for the morning after.

INGREDIENTS

1	ginger juice, freshly squeezed	15 ml (½ oz)
2	premium vodka	60 ml (2 oz)
3	apple juice, freshly squeezed	30 ml (1 oz)
4	Simple Sour Mix (page 41)	15 ml (½ oz)
5	Chilli Syrup (page 40)	dash
6	ginger slice	to garnish

EQUIPMENT Juicer, shaker, strainer

METHOD Add the liquids to a shaker and shake with ice. Add more syrup to taste. Strain into a coupe and garnish with a slice of fresh ginger.

GLASS TYPE:
COUPE

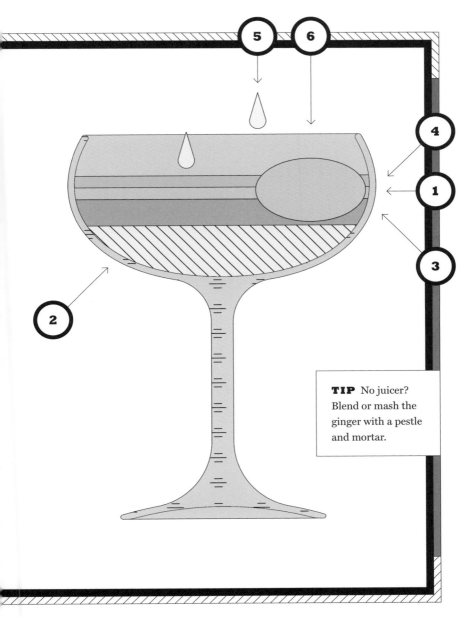

TIP No juicer? Blend or mash the ginger with a pestle and mortar.

INDEX

143

ABOUT
DAN JONES

Perhaps the world's most prolific cocktail enjoyer and author of several books in the *Shake, Muddle, Stir* series, including *Gin, Rum* and *Tequila*, as well as *The Mixer's Manual* and *The Big Book of Gin*, Dan Jones is a writer and editor living in London. A self-professed homebody, he is well versed in the art of at-home drinking and loves to entertain, constantly researching his cocktail craft and trying out new recipes.